# Read All About It

## Book 1

Lori Howard

OXFORD
UNIVERSITY PRESS

Oxford University Press
198 Madison Avenue, New York, NY 10016 USA
Great Clarendon Street, Oxford OX2 6DP England

*Oxford New York*
*Athens Auckland Bangkok Bogota Buenos Aires Calcutta*
*Cape Town Chennai Dar es Salaam Delhi Florence Hong Kong*
*Istanbul Karachi Kuala Lumpur Madrid Melbourne*
*Mexico City Mumbai Nairobi Paris São Paulo Singapore*
*Taipei Tokyo Toronto Warsaw*

And associated companies in
*Berlin Ibadan*

OXFORD is a trademark of Oxford University Press.

Copyright © 1999 Oxford University Press

**Library of Congress Cataloging-in-Publication Data**

Howard, Lori (Lori B.)
  Read all about it 1 / Lori Howard.
      p.   cm. — (Oxford picture dictionary series)
  Includes index.
  Summary: Readings based on a variety of materials for adult
and young adult students of English as a second language.
  ISBN 0-19-435196-3 (pbk. : alk. paper)
  1. English language—Textbooks for foreign speakers. 2. Readers.
[1. English language—Textbooks for foreign speakers. 2. Readers.]
I. Title.    II. Title: Read all about it one.    III. Series.
PE1128.H626 1999                                    98-44263
428.2'4—dc21                                              CIP
                                                          AC

**No unauthorized photocopying.**

Editorial Manager: Susan Lanzano
Senior Editor: Amy Cooper
Content Editor: Margot Gramer
Production Editor: Klaus Jekeli
Art Director: Lynn Luchetti
Design Manager: Lynne Torrey
Designer: Nona Reuter
Page Makeup: Keithley and Associates, Inc.
Art Buyer: Tracy Hammond
Picture Researchers: Clare Maxwell and Tracy Hammond
Production Manager: Abram Hall
Production Coordinator: Shanta Persaud
Cover design by Mark C. Kellogg and Shelley Himmelstein

Printing (last digit): 10 9 8 7 6 5 4 3 2 1

Printed in the U.S.A.

*Illustrations by:* Eliot Bergman, Annie Bissett, Carlos Castellanos,
Mary Chandler, John Paul Genzo, Maj-Britt Hagsted, Keithley and
Associates, Inc., Uldis Klavins, Dean Rohrer, Stacey Schuett, Carol
Strebel, Anna Veltfort, Nina Wallace

*The publishers would like to thank the following for their
permission to reproduce photographs:* Nathan Bilow/All Sport;
Philip Barr, Ron Frehm, Itsuo Inouye, Gary Tormontina/AP Photo;
Mark Elias/AP Photo/Birmingham News; AP/Wide World Photo;
Robert Allison/Contact Press Images; Paula Souders/Corbis;
Corbis-Bettman; Gary Hershorn/Corbis-Bettmann; Dick Luria,
Chris Salvo/FPG; Gardens & Historical Museum; History Museums
of San Jose; Ed Lallo, Susan Lapides/Liaison International; Levi
Strauss & Co. Archives; courtesy of Mall of America; Mobile Press
Register/Gamma Liaison Network; William Munoz; courtesy of
NASA; Lucian Perkins; Dr. Jeremy Burgess/Photo Researchers;
courtesy of the San Francisco Circus School; Lawrence Migdale/
Stock Boston/PNI; Ron Cohn, Koko/The Gorilla Foundation;
Daemmrich, Townsend P. Dickinson, N.R. Roman, M. Siluk/The
Image Works; David Ball, Jon Feingersh, Don Mason, John Olson,
Randy O'Rourke, Kunio Owaki/The Stock Market; Amwell, David
Hanover/Tony Stone Images; UPI/Corbis-Bettmann

*The publishers would also like to thank the following for their help:*
For the Ann Landers reading, permission granted by Ann Landers
    and Creators Syndicate.
"Portrait by a Neighbour" reprinted from *Collected Poems*. New York:
    HarperCollins, copyright 1922, 1950 by Edna St. Vincent Millay.
*This is a Pair of 501 Jeans... The Official History of the Levi's
    Brand*, copyright ©1995. Reprinted with permission from Levi
    Strauss & Co. Archives.
Excerpt from "Window" in *Chicago Poems*, copyright ©1916 by
    Holt, Rinehart and Winston and renewed 1944 by Carl Sandburg,
    reprinted by permission of Harcourt Brace & Company.

*References*
Bondar, Barbara, with Dr. Roberta Bondar, *On the Shuttle: Eight
    Days in Space*. Toronto: Greey de Pencier Books, 1993.
"Consumer Expenditures," *Statistical Abstract of the United States:
    1997*. Washington, DC: US Bureau of the Census, 1997.
"Databank," *Progressive Grocer*. July, 1995, Copyright: Progressive
    Grocer Associates, LLC, 1995.
Howard, Leann, Linda Little, with K. Lynn Savage (Series Editor),
    *Teacher Training Through Video: Problem Solving*. White
    Plains, NY: Longman Publishing Group, 1992.
Johnson, David and Roger Johnson, *Learning Together and Alone:
    Cooperative, Competitive and Individualistic Learning*.
    Englewood Cliffs, NJ: Prentice-Hall, 1987.
Kagan, Spencer, *Cooperative Learning-Resource for Teachers*.
    San Juan Capistrano, CA: Resources for Teachers, 1989.
McMullin, Mary (Series Editor), *Teacher Training Through Video:
    Cooperative Learning*. White Plains, NY: Longman Publishing
    Group, 1993.
NASA Spacelink, http://spacelink.nasa.gov/.index.html
Patent, Dorothy Hinshaw and William Munoz, "Alex, The Talking
    Parrot," *Spider*. Sept. 1996, vol. 3, issue 9, p.19.
Patterson, Francine, "Conversations with a Gorilla," *National
    Geographic*. Oct. 1978.
Peacock, Molly, Elise Paschen, Neil Neches, Editors, *Poetry in
    Motion: 100 Poems from the Subways and Buses*. New York:
    W.W. Norton & Company, Inc., copyright 1996 by MTA New
    York City Transit and the Poetry Society of America.
Public Television Outreach Alliance's Career Exploration Project,
    http://www.pbs.org/jobs
The Gorilla Foundation, http://www.gorilla.org

# TO THE TEACHER

Welcome to the *Read All About It* series.

*Read All About It 1* is a collection of engaging articles, stories, and poems for adult and young adult students of English as a Second or Foreign Language at a high beginning level.

Each of the twelve thematic units in this book contains two high-interest readings based on authentic materials, including news stories, magazine articles, biographies, folktales, and poetry. The readings and activities in each unit focus on one topic such as housing, food, or clothing. This gives students the opportunity to read, listen, speak, and write about one topic in depth and to reinforce and expand their knowledge of related vocabulary. A wide variety of pre-reading, reading, and post-reading activities gives students numerous opportunities to develop cultural awareness as well as problem solving and critical thinking skills. Students will also build reading fluency through the practice of skills such as predicting, skimming, scanning, guessing meaning from context, inferring, and comprehension.

*Read All About It 1* is interactive. Students are encouraged to interact with the text by using their knowledge and experience to help them understand the readings. Students can also interact with each other as they complete the many thought provoking pair and group activities that accompany the readings.

*Read All About It 1* is designed to be flexible and adaptable to the needs of classes and individual students. It can be used as a core reader, as a reading supplement, or for independent study. An accompanying audio tape includes recordings of all the readings. Students who are also using *The Oxford Picture Dictionary* will find that *Read All About It 1* helps bring the *Dictionary* vocabulary to life. Each unit in *Read All About It 1* focuses on the same topic and vocabulary as the corresponding unit in *The Oxford Picture Dictionary* and incorporates vocabulary from other units as well.

Students who use *Read All About It 1* will gain confidence in their reading ability and learn that they can understand what they read without knowing every word. The strategies they learn will help them to enjoy reading and encourage them to read more.

## Tour of a Unit

**TALK ABOUT IT**, usually led by the teacher, is aimed at introducing the topic, motivating the students, and encouraging them to share their prior knowledge about it. The open-ended activities presented in this section allow students of varying abilities to participate and benefit. They can share their personal experiences through guided discussions with classmates.

**READ ABOUT IT** includes pre-reading, reading, and post-reading activities. Although many activities direct students to work in pairs or small groups, almost all of the activities can be done individually.

*Before You Read* asks students to gather more specific information about the upcoming passage just as competent readers do. Students look at illustrations or photos that accompany the reading, as well as the title and headings, and make predictions about the reading. New vocabulary is introduced in context and, in many cases, is evident in the captions of the pictures. *Before You Read* can be teacher-led or done individually and then discussed with the whole group.

*While You Read* focuses students on the reading and asks them to reflect on their pre-reading predictions as they read silently. Students are not expected to understand every word; they should be encouraged to read for the general meaning and to use context clues and their background knowledge to aid comprehension. Readings increase slightly in length and complexity as students progress. Activities include:

▶ *What did you read?* Students are asked to identify the main idea of the reading.

▶ **_Read again_** provides students with a second opportunity to read the whole passage or parts of the passage silently, focusing on a set of comprehension questions.

▶ **_Show you understand_** asks students to demonstrate their comprehension of the passage in a variety of ways such as using vocabulary in context, categorizing, sequencing ideas, and making inferences.

▶ **_Talk more about it_** invites students to relate the material they have read to their own experience and knowledge and use it to discuss ideas, history, and/or culture. Depending on their level of fluency, students may offer short answers or delve more deeply into the questions with longer discussions.

**_After You Read_** helps students to further develop their reading skills and vocabulary. Students practice writing, which supports and reinforces the reading. Depending on the time available, these activities can be either done in class or assigned for homework.

**READ MORE ABOUT IT** offers an opportunity for students to read further about the same topic. Shorter than READ ABOUT IT, it is similar in format and includes many of the same kinds of activities.

## Special Features

**Teacher's Notes**
Teacher's Notes include general information about using this book, specific information about each unit, and suggested extension activities.

**Answer Key**
A removable Answer Key is available for individuals to check their work. However, when students are working in pairs or small groups, they should be encouraged to check their answers with each other to maximize peer interaction. This flexibility makes _Read All About It 1_ useful in classroom, laboratory, and home settings alike.

**Word List**
A unit-by-unit word list provides _Oxford Picture Dictionary_ page references for vocabulary used in this book, so that students who have the _Dictionary_ can use it for support. Teachers can also use the list to determine which words in the readings appear in the _Dictionary_.

**Remember the Words**
A personal vocabulary diary helps students learn new words of their choice.

I hope you and your students enjoy _Read All About It 1_, and I welcome your comments and ideas.

Write to me at:
Oxford University Press, ESL Department
198 Madison Avenue, New York, New York 10016

_Lori Howard_

### Author's Acknowledgments

_The author would like to thank the following people for their helpful reviews of the manuscript:_ Gretchen Bitterlin, Steven Blakesly, Laurie Ehrenhalt, Joyce Grabowski, Maggie Grennan, Eliza Jensen, Alena Mankovecky, Dian Perkins, Michelle Rodgers-Amini, Jean Rose, Stephanie Shipp, Stephen Sloan, Connie Tucker, Zirka Vironka

_The contributions of the following people are deeply appreciated:_
Susan Lanzano, Editorial Manager, who had confidence in me from the outset of this project.
Amy Cooper, Senior Editor, a master of the art of editing who nurtured and shared in the creative process.
Klaus Jekeli, Production Editor, who painstakingly reviewed the manuscript with good judgment and good humor.
Justin Hartung for his tireless work on the many details of this project.
Clare Maxwell and Tracy Hammond, whose photo research turned up many treasures.
Nan Clarke for her editorial expertise.

Much gratitude goes to Jayme Adelson-Goldstein and Norma Shapiro for their invaluable suggestions and their unwavering support.

_Many thanks go to my colleagues, friends, and family members,_ especially Julie Bernard, Jan Hunter, Kathleen Piraino, Yoko Nakajima, Jan Schrumpf, Cristina Schrumpf, Debbie Sistino, Steve Sloan, Robert Werner, and Len Wolff. And to my mentors Fred Reckker, Sadae Iwataki, Greta Kojima, Bob Rumin, K. Lynn Savage, Mary McMullin, Leann Howard, my colleagues at the ESL Teacher Institute, and my wonderful students.

_Thanks also go to the following individuals and organizations who provided their expertise:_ The reference librarians of the San Francisco and Mill Valley Public Libraries and the Marin County Free Libraries; Mall of America; Winchester Mystery House; Lynn Downey, Historian, Levi Strauss & Company; Martin Rayman, DDS; Charlotte Toothman; KPIX TV, San Francisco.

This book is lovingly dedicated to my husband, Greg Wolff, whose encouragement, counsel, and patience made this project possible and to our children, Eric and Lindsay, who inspired me with their stories and supported me with their love.

# CONTENTS

## TALK ABOUT IT

**A. Work with a partner. Look at the pictures. Circle the answers.**

| | | |
|---|---|---|
| **1.** Rosa wants to buy | **a.** a dress. | **b.** a sweater. |
| **2.** Rosa pays | **a.** $49. | **b.** $59. |
| **3.** The same sweater at Deb's Dresses costs | **a.** $49. | **b.** $35. |

**B. Think about these questions. Then ask and answer the questions with your partner.**

> **1.** How do you think Rosa feels?
>
> **2.** What do you think Rosa is going to do now?
>
> **3.** Did Rosa's problem ever happen to you? How did you feel? What did you do?

# READ ABOUT IT

## Before You Read

**Look at the pictures. Look at the title of the reading. Guess what is happening in the pictures. Circle your guesses.**

Picture **1**    A poor man is smelling / buying bread.

Picture **2**    The baker is happy / angry.

Picture **3**    The baker gets / doesn't get money.

## While You Read

**Read this folktale. Think about your guesses while you read.**

### The Smell of Bread

A baker lives in a small town. Every day he makes bread at his bakery. His thick, brown bread is delicious. It has a wonderful smell.

Every morning Gabriel sits down in front of the bakery and smells the bread. Gabriel is a poor man. He doesn't have enough money to buy the bread, but he loves the smell.

One winter day the baker sees Gabriel smelling the bread. He gets very angry. "You are stealing the smell of my bread," he says. "You can't do that! You must pay me for it!" "I'm not eating the bread," answers Gabriel. "I don't have to pay just to smell it." "Yes, you do," says the baker. "Let's ask the judge," says Gabriel.

The judge listens to Gabriel and the baker. "This is a difficult problem," he says. He sits and thinks. After two hours the judge asks Gabriel, "Do you have any money?" Gabriel takes out a little bag with ten pennies in it. "Shake the bag, Gabriel," says the judge. Gabriel shakes the bag and the coins jingle. "Listen to the sound of the coins, Baker," says the judge. "The sound of Gabriel's money pays for the smell of your bread."

### ▶ Read again

**Are these sentences true? Find the answers in the reading. Circle *yes* or *no*.**
**Check your answers with a partner.**

1. The bread smells good.          (yes)     no

2. Gabriel buys bread every day.      yes     no

3. Gabriel steals the bread.         yes     no

4. The baker wants money for the smell of the bread.     yes     no

5. Gabriel has some money.         yes     no

6. Gabriel gives some money to the baker.     yes     no

### ▶ Show you understand

**Put these sentences in order. Number them from 1–5. Then retell the story**
**to your partner. Add other details you remember.**

_____ The baker wants money for the smell of the bread.

_____ The judge says, "The sound of the money pays for the smell of the bread."

_____ Gabriel doesn't want to pay.

__1__ Gabriel smells the bread.

_____ Gabriel and the baker ask the judge for help.

### ▶ Talk more about it

**Think about these questions. Then discuss your ideas.**

1. Is the baker a good man? Why or why not?

2. Do you agree with the judge? Why or why not?

3. Do you know a story like this one? Tell it to your partner.
   What is different about the two stories?

## After You Read

▶ *Words, words, words*

**Read these sentences. Look at the <u>underlined</u> words. What do they mean? Circle *a* or *b*.**

**1.** His thick, brown bread is <u>delicious</u>. It has a <u>wonderful</u> smell.

| *delicious* means | **ⓐ** tastes good | **b.** tastes bad |
| *wonderful* means | **a.** good | **b.** bad |

**2.** "You are <u>stealing</u> the smell of my bread," he says. "You must pay me for it!"

| *stealing* means | **a.** buying something | **b.** taking something that is not yours |

**3.** "<u>Shake</u> the bag, Gabriel," says the judge. Gabriel shakes the bag and the coins <u>jingle</u>. "Listen to the sound of the coins, Baker," says the judge.

| *shake* means | **a.** hold it still | **b.** move it up and down |
| *jingle* means | **a.** make a sound | **b.** move around |

▶ *Write*

**Choose new words for the story. Circle them. Then copy this new story on your own paper.**

---

Good Smells

<u>Yoko / Daniel</u> smells the <u>cookies / chicken</u> at a <u>bakery / restaurant</u>. The <u>baker / cook</u> wants money for the smell. <u>Yoko / Daniel</u> doesn't want to pay. They ask the <u>judge / police officer</u> for help.

<u>Yoko / Daniel</u> shakes a <u>bag / box</u> of coins. The <u>judge / police officer</u> says, "The sound of the <u>money / coins</u> pays for the smell of the <u>cookies / chicken</u>."

---

## READ MORE ABOUT IT

### Before You Read

**Look at the pictures. Look at the title of the reading. Guess the answers to the questions. Circle them.**

1. What is the man holding?

    **a.** a credit card and a postcard     **b.** an ID card and a letter

2. What is the man talking about?

    **a.** some bills he is going to pay     **b.** some prizes he is going to win

### While You Read

**Read this magazine article. Think about your guesses while you read.**

# You Are a Winner!

One evening David Johnson gets home from work and opens his mailbox. In the mailbox he finds this postcard.

David is excited. He wants the prizes. David looks at the telephone number on the postcard. It's a long-distance call, but he dials the number. A woman answers the phone. "Congratulations!" she says. "You win!"

David wins many prizes. He wins a color TV and some gold jewelry. He also wins 100 dolls. The woman says, "You must pay the cost of sending the prizes. It costs $395.00." David thinks that it is very expensive, but he wants the prizes. He uses his credit card to pay the $395.00.

David is happy. He's going to give the jewelry to his wife. He's going to give the dolls to his little girl for her birthday. He can't wait for the prizes to come.

The next week David gets two small, light boxes in the mail. David opens the boxes and he is very surprised. The 100 dolls come in a little box. Each doll is very small — only 1 inch (2.54 cm) tall. The jewelry is not real gold and the TV is a toy. David is angry. He paid $395.00 for nothing! He lost his money!

## ▶ Read again

**Complete these sentences. Find the answers in the reading. Circle *a* or *b*. Check your answers with a partner.**

1. David opens      **a.** a letter.      **b.** the mailbox.
2. He finds      **a.** a postcard.      **b.** a check.
3. David wins      **a.** one prize.      **b.** many prizes.
4. Sending the prizes costs      **a.** no money.      **b.** a lot of money.
5. He pays      **a.** by credit card.      **b.** by check.
6. The prizes are      **a.** good.      **b.** bad.

## ▶ Show you understand

**Do you agree with these sentences? Mark (X) your answers. Talk about your answers with your partner. Then discuss your ideas with the class.**

### What Do You Think?

|  | YES | MAYBE | NO |
|---|---|---|---|
| 1. Many people get postcards from XYZ Company. |  |  |  |
| 2. All the people win prizes. |  |  |  |
| 3. XYZ Company charges too much money for sending the prizes. |  |  |  |
| 4. XYZ Company sends good prizes. |  |  |  |
| 5. XYZ Company makes a lot of money. |  |  |  |
| 6. David should call the police. |  |  |  |

## ▶ Talk more about it

**Think about these questions. Then discuss your ideas.**

1. Is the XYZ Company a good company? Why or why not?
2. Did you ever get a postcard like David's? What did you do?
3. Did you ever win a prize? What was it? How did you win it?

 **Turn to *Remember the Words*, page 105.**

## TALK ABOUT IT

**A. Work with a partner. Look at the pictures of twins. Do they look the same or different? Mark (X) your answers in the chart below.**

Matthew and Melvin Lete

Jennifer and Jill Smith

| | SAME | DIFFERENT |
|---|---|---|
| hair | | |
| clothing | | |
| height | | |
| weight | | |

| | SAME | DIFFERENT |
|---|---|---|
| hair | | |
| clothing | | |
| height | | |
| weight | | |

**B. Look at the pictures again. Describe one pair of twins to your partner. Your partner will describe the other pair to you.**

Example:    *Matthew and Melvin are the same weight.*
            *Jennifer has shoulder-length hair, but Jill has short hair.*

**C. In the picture on the left, Matthew looks like Melvin. Who do you look like? Circle your answers. You can circle more than one. Then talk about your answers with a partner.**

1. I look like my

   **a.** father    **b.** mother    **c.** sister    **d.** brother    **e.** _____

2. We have the same

   **a.** eyes    **b.** nose    **c.** chin    **d.** mouth    **e.** hair color    **f.** _____

# READ ABOUT IT

## Before You Read

Look at the picture and the words under the picture. Look at the title of the reading. Guess the answers to the questions. Circle them.

1. What is this reading about?  **a.** best friends    **b.** twin sisters

2. What do the women like?  **a.** the same things    **b.** different things

## While You Read

Read this magazine article. Think about your guesses while you read.

# Two of a Kind

Isobel and Betty Rickets are twins. Almost everything about these middle-aged sisters is the same. They both have short, wavy black hair, brown eyes, and round faces. They both are of average height and weight and wear glasses. They always wear the same clothing, too. **1**

Isobel and Betty live next door to each other. Their houses look the same. The houses have the same floor plan and the same furniture. The furniture is in the same place in both houses. Only one thing is different about the houses — the addresses. **2**

Isobel's and Betty's clothing looks alike, their houses look alike, and their husbands look alike, too. They are married to twin brothers. Their husbands' names are Marty and Mackall. Each couple has three children. The children are cousins, but they feel like brothers and sisters. **3**

Isobel and Betty never feel lonely because they spend a lot of time with each other. Twice a week they go to the market and cook dinner together. On weekends they like to go shopping together. They even have the same hobby. Isobel and Betty collect dolls — twin dolls, of course! **4**

**Isobel and Betty have the same hobby. They collect dolls.**

## ▶ *What did you read?*

**What is this reading about? Circle the best answer.**

**a.** Isobel and Betty like to be twins.     **b.** Isobel and Betty don't like to be twins.

## ▶ *Read again*

**Look at this chart. Find the answers in the reading. Mark (X) them.**
**Check your answers with a partner.**

| Isobel and Betty | SAME | DIFFERENT |
|---|---|---|
| 1. clothing | X | |
| 2. hair color | | |
| 3. address | | |
| 4. husband's name | | |
| 5. hobby | | |

## ▶ *Show you understand*

**Complete these sentences. Use the words on the left to help you. Then retell**
**the story about Isobel and Betty to your partner. Add other details you remember.**

**hair color**

**eye color**

**furniture**

**number of children**

**hobby**

1. They have the same _____hair color_____.

2. They have _____.

3. They _____.

4. _____.

5. And they _____.

## ▶ *Talk more about it*

**Think about these questions. Then discuss your ideas.**

1. When Isobel, Betty, Marty, and Mackall go out together, other people often look at them. Why? How do you think the couples feel?

2. Some people think twins should live different lives. What do you think? Should they wear different clothing? Should they live in different towns? Why or why not?

## After You Read

### ▶ Skim for the topic

**Skim the reading. What is each paragraph about?
Draw a line from the paragraph to the topic.**

skim = read quickly to get
the general idea

| Paragraph | Topic |
| --- | --- |
| Paragraph **1** | Hobbies and Activities |
| Paragraph **2** | Physical Description |
| Paragraph **3** | Family |
| Paragraph **4** | Houses |

### ▶ Write

**A. Circle the questions you want to ask Isobel and Betty. Write one question of your own.**

1. Where do you live?

2. What are your children's names?

3. Are any of your children twins?

4. How many dolls do you have?

5. _____ ?

**B. Write a letter to Isobel and Betty. Copy the letter on your own paper and write in your questions.**

Dear Isobel and Betty,

I read a story about your lives. I want to know more about you.

Write your questions here.

Sincerely,

Sign your name.

 **EXTRA! EXTRA!** Every August 3,000 pairs of twins go to the Twins Day Festival in Twinsburg, Ohio.

**Getting Married**

Getting engaged

Buying wedding veils

Having a double wedding

## Before You Read

**Look at the pictures and the words under the pictures. Look at the title of the reading. Guess the answer to the question. Circle it.**

What is this reading about?   **a.** sisters getting married   **b.** buying wedding clothes

## While You Read

**Read this newspaper column. Think about your guess while you read.**

# A Double Wedding

Dear Readers:

In 1939 my twin sister and I were both engaged. We were excited because we planned to get married at the same time in a double wedding. I was engaged to a law student from Los Angeles. My sister was engaged to a student from the University of Minnesota.

One day we were in a department store to buy our wedding veils. The manager of the women's hat department put a veil in my hands. The veil was beautiful. I liked it. The manager was attractive. I liked him. We fell in love.

The double wedding was on July 2, the day we planned. But I did not marry the law student. My new husband was the manager of the hat department!

**ANN LANDERS**

My sister is still married to her Minnesota sweetheart. My husband and I got divorced after 36 years of marriage. Isn't life interesting?

—Ann Landers

## ► Read again

**Are these sentences true? Find the answers in the reading. Circle *yes* or *no*. Check your answers with a partner.**

1. Ann has a twin sister.      (yes)    no
2. Ann bought her wedding veil from a man.      yes    no
3. Ann and her sister got married at the same time.      yes    no
4. Ann married a law student.      yes    no
5. Ann is still married to the store manager.      yes    no

## ► Show you understand

**Fill in the blanks with words from the box.**

| engaged | ~~twin~~ | married | divorced | double |
|---------|------|---------|----------|--------|

Ann and her _____*twin*_____ sister planned a _____ wedding.

Ann was _____ to a law student, but she _____

the manager of a hat department. Ann's sister is still married,

but Ann got _____.

## ► Talk more about it

**Think about these questions. Then discuss your ideas.**

1. Ann was engaged to a law student, but she didn't marry him. How do you think he felt about that? How do you think she felt?

2. Ann met her husband in a department store. In your country, where do people usually meet their husbands or wives?

3. Ann got divorced after 36 years of marriage. Talk about divorce in your country. How many couples get divorced? Why do they get divorced?

 **Turn to *Remember the Words*, page 105.**

# Home Sweet Home

## TALK ABOUT IT

**A. Work with a partner. Look at the pictures. Guess the answers to the questions. Fill in the chart.**

| | | | | |
|---|---|---|---|---|
| **1.** What kind of home is this? | a mansion | | | |
| **2.** Where is it? | | | | |
| **3.** How many bedrooms and bathrooms do you think it has? | | | | |
| **4.** Who do you think lives here? | | | | |

**B. Think about these questions. Then ask and answer the questions with your partner.**

1. What kind of place do you like to live in? A house? An apartment? Why?

2. Where do you like to live? In the city? In the country? Why?

The Winchester Mystery House in San Jose, California

Sarah and William Winchester

Carpenters worked 24 hours a day for 38 years.

## Before You Read

Look at the pictures and the words near the pictures. Look at the title of the reading. Guess the answers to the questions. Circle them.

**1.** What is this reading about?

    **a.** A woman bought a large house.    **b.** A woman built a large house.

**2.** Who lived in the house?

    **a.** a married couple and 6 children    **b.** a woman

**3.** When does the story begin?

    **a.** 1861                  **b.** 1961

# SARAH WINCHESTER AND THE
# MYSTERY HOUSE

One day in 1861 Sarah Pardee met William Winchester in the small town of New Haven, Connecticut. She was from a fine family. He was the son of the president of the Winchester Gun Company. William and Sarah fell in love and got married a year later. They were happy together, but only for a few years.

A Winchester gun

**1.** What happened next?

   **a.** Sarah and William bought a house.     **b.** William died.

In 1866 Sarah and William had a baby daughter. Their little baby got sick and died 40 days later. They were very sad. Then in 1881 William got tuberculosis and died. Sarah was very upset. The two most important people in her life were dead. One day a woman came to see Sarah. The woman said, "I can tell you about the future."

**2.** What did the woman tell Sarah?

   **a.** "Don't be sad."     **b.** "You must go to California."

"Your daughter and husband died," said the woman. "Do you want to die, too?" she asked. "No," said Sarah. "Then you must do two things," said the woman. "First, move to California. Then, build a house. And remember, don't stop building or you will die!"

**3.** What did Sarah do?

    **a.** She stayed in Connecticut.    **b.** She moved to California.

Sarah was scared. She packed everything and moved west to California in 1884. She bought some land and started to build a house. Carpenters worked on the house 24 hours a day for 38 years. In 1922 Sarah died and the work finally stopped.

**4.** What does the house look like now? Circle the right numbers.

The house has

    **a.** 20 / 40 bedrooms.    **b.** 1 / 6 kitchens.    **c.** 10 / 47 fireplaces.

Sarah's mansion still stands in San Jose, California. People visit the Winchester Mystery House every day. The house has 160 rooms. It has 40 bedrooms, 6 kitchens, and 40 stairways. There are 1,257 windows and 950 doors. To keep the house warm there are 47 fireplaces and 19 chimneys. The house is big. It is also strange. Some stairways go nowhere. They end at a ceiling. Some doors open into walls. Why did Sarah Winchester build such a strange house? No one knows. It's a mystery!

This stairway goes nowhere.

## ▶ Read again

**Are these sentences true? Find the answers in the reading. Circle _yes_ or _no_.**
**Check your answers with a partner.**

1. People can visit the Winchester Mystery House.     (yes)     no

2. The house is in Colorado.     yes     no

3. Carpenters worked on the house for 24 years.     yes     no

4. The house has 160 rooms.     yes     no

5. The house has 1,257 doors.     yes     no

## ▶ Show you understand

**A. Put these sentences in order. Number them from 1–6.**

___1___ Sarah and William got married.     _____ She built a house.

_____ Sarah moved west.     _____ They had a baby.

_____ The baby died.     _____ William died.

**B. Copy the sentences above in order. Retell the story to your partner.**
**Use _First_, _Then_, and _Finally_ to show the order of the story. Add other**
**details you remember.**

1. First, _____Sarah and William got married._____

2. Then, _____they_____

3. Then, _____

4. Then, _____

5. Then, _____

6. Finally, _____

## ▶ Talk more about it

**Think about these questions. Then discuss your ideas.**

1. Sarah moved to California after her husband and baby died.
   Do you know someone who moved away? Why did he or she move?

2. A woman told Sarah about the future. Do you believe people can
   tell about the future? Why or why not?

# After You Read

## ▶ Pronouns

**Look at the circled words. What do they mean? Draw an arrow to the words that tell the meaning.**

1. One day in 1861 Sarah Pardee met William Winchester in the small town of New Haven, Connecticut. (He) was the son of the president of the Winchester Gun Company.

2. In 1866 Sarah and William had a baby daughter. Their little baby got sick and died 40 days later. (They) were very sad.

3. Sarah was scared. (She) packed everything and moved west to California.

4. The house has 160 rooms. (It) has 40 bedrooms, 6 kitchens, and 40 stairways.

5. Some stairways go nowhere. (They) end at a ceiling.

## ▶ Puzzle

**Read these sentences. Find the words in the box that go in each blank. Write the words in the puzzle. Follow the example.**

| chimneys | ~~upset~~ | future | stairways | mystery | gun | daughter |
|---|---|---|---|---|---|---|

1. Sarah's husband died, and she was ____ .

2. The house has 40 bedrooms and 40 ____ .

3. A woman visited Sarah. She told Sarah about the ____ .

4. Sarah and William had a baby ____ .

5. There are 19 ____ in the Winchester House.

6. William's father was the president of a ____ company.

7. Why do some stairways go nowhere? No one knows. It's a ____ .

1. <u>u</u> <u>p</u> <u>s</u> <u>e</u> <u>t</u>
2. ___ ___ ___ ___ ___ ___ ___ ___ ___
3. ___ ___ ___ ___ ___ ___
4. ___ ___ ___ ___ ___ ___ ___ ___
5. ___ ___ ___ ___ ___ ___ ___
6. ___ ___ ___
7. ___ ___ ___ ___ ___ ___ ___

**What is the secret word?** _____

# READ MORE ABOUT IT

## Before You Read

Look at the pictures. Look at the reading and the title of the reading. Guess the answers to the questions. Circle them.

**1.** What kind of reading is this?

   **a.** a story        **b.** a poem        **c.** a newspaper column

**2.** Who lives in the house?

   **a.** a young woman    **b.** a middle-aged woman    **c.** an elderly woman

## While You Read

Read this selection aloud. Think about your guesses while you read.

# Portrait by a Neighbor
### Edna St. Vincent Millay

**I**  Before she has her floor swept
Or her dishes done,
Any day you'll find her
A-sunning in the sun!

**II**  It's long after midnight
Her key's in the lock,
And you never see her chimney smoke
Till past ten o'clock!

**III**  She digs in her garden
With a shovel and a spoon,
She weeds her lazy lettuce
By the light of the moon.

**IV**  Her lawn looks like a meadow,
And if she mows the place
She leaves the clover standing
And the Queen Anne's lace!

## ▶ *Read again*

**Complete these sentences. Find the answers in the reading. Circle *a* or *b*.
Check your answers with a partner.**

1. She sits in the sun     **a.** before she cleans her house.     **b.** after she cleans her house.

2. She gets home       **a.** early.               **b.** late.

3. She wakes up        **a.** early.               **b.** late.

4. She weeds her garden    **a.** at night.           **b.** in the daytime.

5. She mows her lawn      **a.** often.             **b.** sometimes.

## ▶ *Show you understand*

**Read aloud part I of the poem on page 19. In the second and fourth lines, the last
words rhyme (have the same sound). Listen for the rhyme. Read aloud the rest
of the poem. Write the words that rhyme in the blanks.**

I    _____*done*_____ rhymes with _____*sun*_____

II   _____ rhymes with _____

III   _____ rhymes with _____

IV   _____ rhymes with _____

## ▶ *Write*

**Write about your neighbor on your own paper. Use these questions and the
example to help you.**

1. What kind of home does your neighbor live in?

2. What does she or he like to do? Name two things.

3. When does she or he get home at night?

4. When does she or he wake up in the morning?

*My neighbor lives in an apartment. He likes to wash his
car every Saturday. He also likes to listen to music. He gets
home late at night, and he wakes up early in the morning.*

 **Turn to *Remember the Words*, page 105.**

## TALK ABOUT IT

**A. Work in a small group. Read the graph. Answer the question.**

Money People in the U.S. Spend on Fruit and Vegetables

Dollars spent each week

$5.00 / 4.00 / 3.00 / 2.00 / 1.00 / 0

Fresh    Canned    Frozen

How much do people in the United States spend on fruit and vegetables each week?

|  FRESH  |  CANNED  |  FROZEN  |  TOTAL SPENT  |
|---------|----------|----------|---------------|
| 1. $5.00 | 2. _____ | 3. _____ | 4. _____ |

**B. Fill in the graph.**

Money You Spend on Fruit and Vegetables

Dollars spent each week

$5.00 / 4.00 / 3.00 / 2.00 / 1.00 / 0

Fresh    Canned    Frozen

**C. Ask and answer these questions with a partner.**

**1.** How much do you spend on fruit and vegetables each week?

**2.** Where do you buy your fruit and vegetables—at the supermarket, corner store, farmers' market, or fruit stand? Why?

# READ ABOUT IT

## Before You Read

**Look at the pictures and the words under the pictures. Look at the title of the reading. Guess the answers to the questions.**

**1.** Where is the man?     **a.** at a supermarket     **b.** at a farmers' market

**2.** What is he selling? _____

## While You Read

**Read this newspaper article. Think about your guesses while you read.**

# Fresh is Best

Greg Martinez sells fresh fruit and vegetables at a New York City market.

The sun is shining. Music is playing. The smell of raspberries is in the air. It's fall at a farmers' market in New York City. Greg Martinez is selling the fruit and vegetables he grows on his farm—potatoes, apples, cauliflower, and carrots. People are walking by—looking, tasting, and buying.

Today Greg and many other farmers sell their fruit and vegetables at farmers' markets around the city. In 1976 there was only one farmers' market in New York City. Now there are 27. In 1976 there were only 100 farmers' markets in the United States, but now there are more than 2,500.

For hundreds of years everyone shopped at farmers' markets in cities and towns around the country. Things changed after World War II. Many people moved from the cities to new suburbs. In the suburbs, business people built big markets. At these supermarkets people could buy fresh, frozen, canned, and packaged foods. They could buy almost everything they needed. People didn't need farmers' markets anymore.

Now farmers' markets are coming back to cities and towns. Why do people go to farmers' markets? The food is fresh, ripe, and tastes great. The lovely smell of fresh produce is everywhere. Farmers' markets often have many new and different kinds of foods. For example,

there are white potatoes, yellow potatoes, and even purple potatoes! The prices are good, too. Usually it is cheaper to shop at a farmers' market. Also, many shoppers like to talk to the farmers about the food they grow. It's fun to go to a farmers' market! ■

## ▶ What did you read?

**What is this reading about? Circle the best answer.**

**a.** fresh produce      **b.** farmers' markets

## ▶ Read again

**Are these sentences true? Find the answers in the reading. Circle *yes* or *no*. Check your answers with a partner.**

1. Many farmers sell their fruit and vegetables at farmers' markets in New York City.     (yes)    no

2. Now the United States has only 100 farmers' markets.     yes    no

3. After World War II many people shopped at farmers' markets.     yes    no

4. Now many cities and towns in the United States have farmers' markets.     yes    no

5. People shop at farmers' markets because the food is fresh, ripe, and tastes great.     yes    no

## ▶ Show you understand

**Answer the questions. Mark (X) the correct boxes. Use the reading to help you.**

| | FARMERS' MARKETS | SUPERMARKETS |
|---|---|---|
| 1. Where does the sun shine? | X | |
| 2. Where can you taste fruit and vegetables? | | |
| 3. Where can you buy everything you need? | | |
| 4. Where is it more expensive to shop? | | |
| 5. Where can you talk to farmers? | | |

## ▶ Talk more about it

**Think about these questions. Then discuss your ideas.**

1. Do you like to go to farmers' markets? Why or why not?

2. Are there farmers' markets in your country? How often can you go? What can you buy?

## After You Read

▶ *Words, words, words*

**Read these sentences. Look at the underlined words. They are not correct.**
**Draw lines to the correct words.**

**1.** Greg Martinez is selling the <u>rice</u>...

**2.** ...and vegetables he <u>eats</u> on his farm.

**3.** People are walking by—looking, tasting, and <u>selling</u>.

**4.** In the suburbs, business people built <u>small</u> markets.

**5.** The food is fresh, <u>rotten</u>, and tastes great.

**6.** Usually it is <u>more expensive</u> to shop at a farmers' market.

**a.** grows

**b.** buying

**c.** fruit

**d.** ripe

**e.** cheaper

**f.** large

▶ *Write*

**Write about a vegetable or fruit dish from your country. Use these questions and**
**the example to help you. Write on your own paper.**

**1.** What is your favorite vegetable or fruit dish?

**2.** What is in it?

**3.** Is it a cold or a hot dish?

**4.** Why is it your favorite?

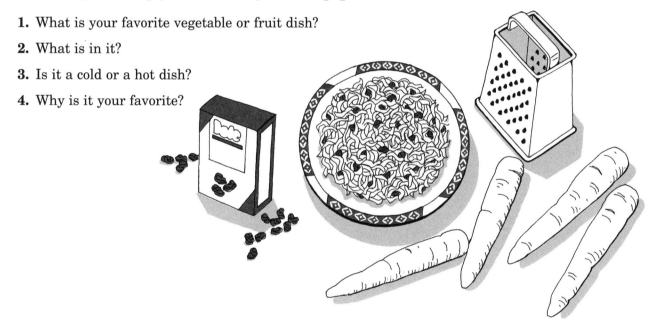

*My favorite vegetable dish is carrot salad. It has lots of*
*grated carrots, a few raisins, and a little mayonnaise. It's a*
*cold dish. It's my favorite because I love carrots.*

 The most popular fruit in the world is the mango.

# READ MORE ABOUT IT

## Before You Read

**A. Look at the pictures and the title of the reading. Skim the reading. Circle the best answer.**

What kind of reading is this?

**a.** a story　　　**b.** a recipe

> skim = read quickly to get the general idea
>
> scan = look quickly to find specific information

**B. How long does it take to make "Purple Potato Salad"? Scan the reading for the times. Write them in the blanks.**

| BOIL POTATOES | COOL POTATOES | BOIL PEAS | TOTAL COOKING TIME |
|---|---|---|---|
| 1. _15 minutes_ | 2. _____ | 3. _____ | 4. _____ |

## While You Read

Read this newspaper article. Check your answers while you read.

### Greg's Purple Potato Salad

Greg Martinez is a farmer and a great cook. He makes delicious dishes with the vegetables he grows. Here is one of his recipes. It uses the purple potatoes from his farm. Try this recipe. Your family and friends will be surprised.

#### Ingredients

1 pound* small purple potatoes (about 10)

1 1/2 quarts** cold water

1 teaspoon salt

3/4 cup*** frozen peas

4 tablespoons Italian salad dressing

2 tablespoons chopped fresh parsley

\* 1 pound = 453.6 grams
\*\* 1 quart = 0.95 liters
\*\*\* 1 cup = 237 milliliters

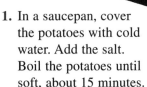

1. In a saucepan, cover the potatoes with cold water. Add the salt. Boil the potatoes until soft, about 15 minutes.

2. With a wooden spoon, move the potatoes to a colander. Drain and cool for 10 minutes.

3. Boil the water again. Boil the peas for 1 minute. Drain the peas in a colander. Rinse with cold water. Drain again and pat dry with a paper towel.

4. Cut the potatoes into quarters.

5. In a bowl, lightly mix the potatoes, peas, salad dressing, and parsley. Add salt and pepper to taste.

Cooking time: 26 minutes.
Makes 4 servings.

## ▶ *Read again*

**Complete these sentences. Find the answers in the reading. Circle *a* or *b*.
Check your answers with a partner.**

1. Greg cooks with vegetables he    **a.** grows.      **b.** buys.

2. Purple Potato Salad has    **a.** potatoes and peas.      **b.** potatoes.

3. To make this dish you need    **a.** 1 quart water.      **b.** 1 ½ quarts water.

4. To make this dish you need    **a.** 2 tablespoons of salad dressing.      **b.** 4 tablespoons of salad dressing.

5. You need these utensils:    **a.** a wooden spoon and a colander.      **b.** a ladle and a strainer.

6. Cut the potatoes    **a.** in half.      **b.** into quarters.

## ▶ *Words, words, words*

**Read these sentences. Look at the <u>underlined</u> words. What do they mean?
Circle *a* or *b*.**

1. <u>Boil</u> the potatoes until soft.    **a.** cook in water using high heat      **b.** cook in water using low heat

2. <u>Drain</u> the peas in a colander.    **a.** put in the drain of the sink      **b.** let the water run off

3. <u>Rinse</u> with cold water.    **a.** run water over      **b.** leave in water

4. Cut the potatoes into <u>quarters</u>.    **a.** little pieces      **b.** 4 equal pieces

5. Add salt and pepper <u>to taste</u>.    **a.** the way you like it      **b.** ½ teaspoon

## ▶ *Talk more about it*

**Think about these questions. Then discuss your ideas.**

1. Do you like to try foods that are new and different?
   Why or why not?

2. In your country, do people make potato salad? What are
   the ingredients? When do people usually eat it?

 **Turn to *Remember the Words*, page 105.**

## TALK ABOUT IT

**A. Look at the pictures. Read the questions in the chart. Circle *yes* or *no*.**
   **Then talk about your answers with a partner. Tell why you answered *yes* or *no*.**

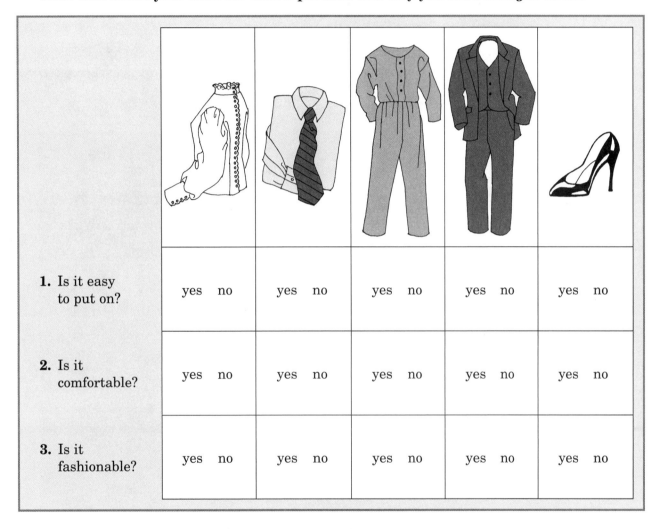

| | | | | | |
|---|---|---|---|---|---|
| **1.** Is it easy to put on? | yes no | yes no | yes no | yes no | yes no |
| **2.** Is it comfortable? | yes no | yes no | yes no | yes no | yes no |
| **3.** Is it fashionable? | yes no | yes no | yes no | yes no | yes no |

**B. Think about these questions. Then ask and answer the questions with your partner.**

> **1.** Which is more important to you—comfortable clothing or fashionable clothing? Why?
>
> **2.** Describe your most comfortable clothing.
>
> **3.** Describe your favorite outfit. Why is it your favorite?

# READ ABOUT IT

## Before You Read

**Look at the pictures and the words next to the pictures. Look at the title of the reading. Guess the answer to the question. Circle it.**

What is this reading about?     **a.** a weed in the fields     **b.** a fastener for clothing

## While You Read

**Read this Web page. Think about your guess while you read.**

# What Will They Think Of Next?

George de Mestral, a Swiss engineer, loved to walk in the country with his dog. But every day after the walk, his pants and the dog's fur were covered with seeds. The seeds came from the cocklebur, a weed in the fields. It was difficult to take the seeds off, and George wanted to know why. He looked at the seeds under a microscope. They looked like small hooks. This gave George an idea.

The cocklebur ▶

George worked for a long time on his idea. After 12 years he made a two-sided fastener. One side had hooks like the seeds. The other side had loops like the material of his pants. In 1958 George started the Velcro Company to sell his new hook and loop fastener.

The Velcro fastener uses hooks and loops. ▶

Now Velcro fasteners are in everything because they make it easier to get dressed. All kinds of clothing use Velcro fasteners instead of buttons, snaps, or zippers. Men's and boys' swimming trunks and shorts use them at the waist. Sandals and athletic shoes use them instead of buckles or shoelaces. Ties, caps, and backpacks often use them, too. Astronauts even use Velcro fasteners in space! They use them to fasten the pockets on their jumpsuits so that small things don't come out.

Velcro fasteners make it easier to get dressed. ▶

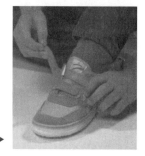

In early times people used rope to fasten their clothing. Later people used buttons, then zippers, and now Velcro fasteners. What will they think of next?

## ▶ *What did you read?*

**Choose another title for the reading. Circle the best one.**

**a.** George de Mestral: A Great Engineer

**b.** Velcro: Its History and Uses

## ▶ *Read again*

**Read these sentences. Look at the reading to find which sentences are correct.**
**Circle *a* or *b*. Check your answers with a partner.**

**1. a.** George walked in the country alone.    **(b.)** George walked in the country with his dog.

**2. a.** After the walk they were covered with seeds.    **b.** After the walk they were covered with dirt.

**3. a.** It was easy to get the seeds off.    **b.** It was difficult to get the seeds off.

**4. a.** George made a new kind of seed.    **b.** George made a new kind of fastener.

**5. a.** Velcro fasteners make it easier to get dressed.    **b.** Velcro fasteners make it more difficult to get dressed.

## ▶ *Show you understand*

**Look at this chart. Find words in the reading that match the categories.**
**Write them in the chart.**

| CLOTHING | SHOES AND ACCESSORIES | FASTENERS |
|---|---|---|
| swimming trunks | sandals | buttons |

## ▶ *Talk more about it*

**Think about these questions. Then discuss your ideas.**

**1.** Velcro fasteners are used in clothing and in products for the home. What things do you have that use Velcro fasteners? Name them.

**2.** How do Velcro fasteners help you?

## After You Read

▶ *Guess the riddle*

**Read these sentences. They describe pieces of clothing and accessories from the reading. Guess the piece of clothing.**

**1.** It is on some shoes.
It is on a belt.
It closes tight.

What is it?  _____a buckle_____

**2.** They have two legs.
They are not people or animals.
You wear them on your legs.

What are they?  _____

**3.** It has pants.
It has a shirt.
It is all one piece.

What is it?  _____

**4.** Men and boys wear them.
They look like shorts.
They can get wet.

What are they?  _____

**5.** You make a knot.
Then you make a bow.
You pull them tight and you can go.

What are they?  _____

**6.** In the summer heat
you wear them on your feet.

What are they?  _____

▶ *Write a riddle*

**Work with a partner. Choose the best words to complete riddles 1 and 2. For 3, write your own riddle about a cap. Use 1 and 2 as examples.**

**1.** You wear it to carry books / read books.
You wear it on your hip / back.

What is it?  _____a backpack_____

**2.** You wear them to _____.

You wear them on your _____.

What are they?  _____athletic shoes_____

**3.** _____.

_____.

_____?  _____a cap_____

# READ MORE ABOUT IT

## Before You Read

**Look at the picture. Look at the title of the reading. Guess the answers to the questions. Circle them.**

**1.** What year is it?       **a.** 1944      **b.** 1984

**2.** Why are these people standing in line?      **a.** to buy pants      **b.** to buy food

## While You Read

**Read this magazine article. Think about your guesses while you read.**

# Jeans Today

It was 1944. The world was at war. It was hard to buy food and clothing.

One day a man broke his leg and went to the hospital. At the hospital the nurse said, "We are going to cut off your jeans. It will hurt too much to pull them off." "No, please don't cut them!" the man said. "Levi's jeans are too hard to find. Pull them off!" So they did. The man had a few minutes of pain, but he still had his jeans. The people at the Levi Strauss Company heard the story and sent the man a free pair of Levi's jeans. They were glad he loved his jeans.

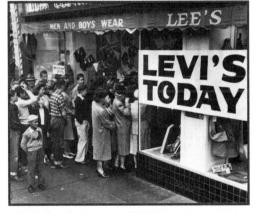

Why do people love their jeans so much? Jeans are very comfortable. They are made of cotton denim material. Every time you wash denim jeans, they get softer and more comfortable. Some companies make other kinds of clothing with the dark blue denim material. It makes the clothing more comfortable. Shorts, overalls, jackets, skirts, hats, and suits are all made of denim. Even formal clothes, like tuxedos and evening gowns, are sometimes made of denim.

All over the world people love jeans. Tight jeans, baggy jeans, striped jeans, plaid jeans; it doesn't matter. From Europe to Asia, from North America to Africa — people buy millions of pairs of jeans every year. In one year they bought 453 million pairs. Put all those jeans in a line and they will go around the world 12 times!

## ▶ Read again

**Are these sentences true? Find the answers in the reading. Circle *yes* or *no*. Then check your answers with a partner.**

| | | |
|---|---|---|
| 1. A man broke his arm. | yes | (no) |
| 2. It was easy to find jeans. | yes | no |
| 3. They cut off his jeans. | yes | no |
| 4. The Levi Strauss Company sent the man some money. | yes | no |
| 5. Jeans are very comfortable. | yes | no |
| 6. Many kinds of clothing are made of denim. | yes | no |
| 7. People buy millions of pairs of jeans every year. | yes | no |

## ▶ Talk more about it

**Think about these questions. Then discuss your ideas.**

1. People love jeans because they are comfortable. What are some other reasons people love jeans?

2. Do you wear jeans? Why or why not?

3. What do you stand in line to buy? How long do you usually stand in line?

## ▶ Write

**Draw a picture of your favorite piece of clothing on your own paper. Then write about it. Use these questions and the example to help you.**

1. What is your favorite piece of clothing?

2. What does it look like?

3. What is it made of?

4. When did you buy it or get it?

5. How often do you wear it?

6. Why do you like it?

My favorite piece of clothing is a sweater. It is a V-neck sweater with long sleeves. It is made of light blue wool. I got it last year. I usually wear it twice a week. I like it because my best friend gave it to me for my birthday.

 **Turn to *Remember the Words*, page 105.**

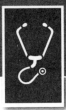
## TALK ABOUT IT

Astronauts must be in excellent health. Before men and women can become astronauts, doctors examine them. Doctors check these things:

| heart | lungs | muscles | bones | blood pressure |

**A. Work with a partner. Label the pictures with words from the box.**

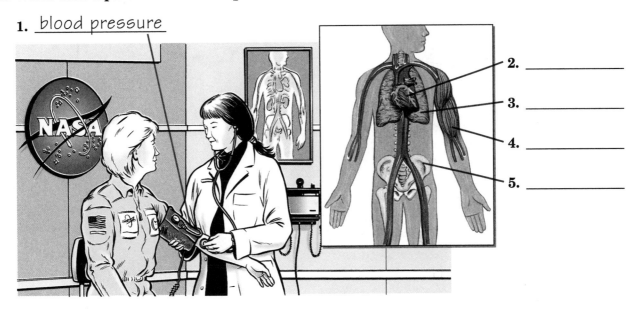

1. blood pressure

2. _____

3. _____

4. _____

5. _____

**B. Can you be an astronaut? Are you healthy? Mark (X) your answers.**

### Rate Your Health

| | GOOD | NEEDS IMPROVEMENT |
|---|---|---|
| 1. heart | | |
| 2. lungs | | |
| 3. muscles | | |
| 4. bones | | |
| 5. blood pressure | | |

**C. How can you improve your health? By exercising? By eating healthy food? Talk about your answers with your partner.**

# READ ABOUT IT

**4...3...2...1...
Blast Off!**

**Astronauts Judy Garcia,
Barbara Morgan,
and Kathleen Beres
float because they
are weightless.**

**Scientists study
changes in the body.**

## *Before You Read*

**Look at the pictures and the words near the pictures. Look at the title and
the subtitles of the reading. Guess the answers to the questions. Circle them.**

**1.** What is this reading about?

    **a.** astronauts' health         **b.** astronauts' work

**2.** What happens to astronauts in space?

    **a.** Their bodies change.         **b.** Their bodies and their brains change.

## While You Read

**Read this textbook page. Think about your guesses while you read.**

# Astronauts in Space

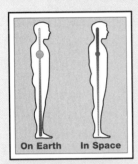
In space, blood in the body moves up to the head.

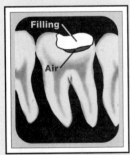
Air under a filling can cause a toothache in space.

This astronaut has motion sickness.

Astronauts blast off into space. In space there is no gravity. The astronauts are weightless. They do not stand or walk—they float. Floating in space changes the astronauts' bodies and brains in many ways. **1**

## Changes in the body

Astronauts' bodies change in space. For example, they get about 1 1/2 inches taller. Their hearts get smaller because the blood in their bodies moves up to their heads. Also, their bones and muscles get weak. To keep their bones and muscles strong, astronauts must exercise 90 minutes every day. In space, astronauts can also have problems with their teeth. Their dental fillings can cause pain. Dentists check the astronauts' teeth before they leave earth. They check for air under the fillings. Air under a filling can cause a toothache in space. **2**

## Changes in the brain

The brain also changes in space. Some of these changes may cause motion sickness. About 65% of astronauts get motion sickness in space. They have many symptoms such as cold skin, sweating, headaches, nausea, and vomiting. Other changes in the brain make it difficult to stand and walk for the first few days back on earth. **3**

Scientists are always studying the changes in the bodies and brains of astronauts. They want to learn how to keep astronauts healthy in space for a long time. Then astronauts could take long trips to visit other planets and maybe even the stars. **4**

**Complete this outline. Find the information in the reading. Then tell your partner about the reading. Use the outline to help you.**

## Astronauts in Space

I. Changes in the body

    A. Astronauts get _____taller_____.

    B. Their hearts get _____.

    C. Their _____ and _____ get weak.

    D. Air under a dental filling can cause a _____.

II. Changes in the brain

    A. About 65% of astronauts get _____ sickness.

    B. It is difficult for some astronauts to _____ and
    _____ for the first few days back on earth.

► *Talk more about it*

**Think about these questions. Then discuss your ideas.**

> **1.** Sometimes astronauts are away from earth for a long time. What do you think they miss? Name three things.
>
> **2.** Do you want to go into space? Why or why not?
>
> **3.** Why is it difficult for some astronauts to walk for the first few days back on earth? Did you ever have trouble walking? What happened?

## After You Read

▶ *Skim for the purpose*

**Skim each paragraph in the reading. Then draw a line from the number of the paragraph to the purpose.**

skim = read quickly to get the general idea

| Paragraph | Purpose |
|---|---|
| Paragraph **1** | tells about changes in the body. |
| Paragraph **2** | tells about changes in the brain. |
| Paragraph **3** | ends the article. |
| Paragraph **4** | begins the article. |

▶ *Words, words, words*

**A. Read the information in the box.**

weight*less* = no weight    An astronaut is weightless in space.

sleep*less* = no sleep    The astronaut had a sleepless night.

**B. Read the sentences. Add *-less* to the words under the lines. Then write the new words in the blanks. Follow the example.**

1. Astronauts float in space. They are ____weightless____.
   **weight**

2. She couldn't sleep on her first night in space. She had a _____ night.
   **sleep**

3. Some food for astronauts has no taste. It is _____.
   **taste**

4. Astronauts eat _____ and _____ chicken, so there is
   **skin**        **bone**
   no waste.

5. Astronauts use a _____ shampoo, so they don't waste water.
   **rinse**

## READ MORE ABOUT IT

### Before You Read

Look at the pictures and the title of the reading. Read this list. Guess which words will be in the reading. Mark (X) them.

_____ electric razor
_____ cologne
_____ shampoo
_____ sink
_____ blowdryer

_____ cut
_____ toothbrush
_____ towel
_____ sunscreen
_____ soap

_____ bath
_____ washcloth
_____ nail polish
_____ wash
_____ sponge

### While You Read

Read this magazine article. Think about your guesses while you read.

# Keeping Clean in Space

Water is weightless in space.

Astronauts have important work to do in space. They must stay healthy to do a good job. Part of staying healthy is keeping clean. Astronauts must take care of their personal hygiene.

But how do astronauts wash themselves in space? Can they take a bath or a shower? No, they can't. On early space flights astronauts tried to take showers, but it didn't work. The water floated all around because water is weightless in space. Now astronauts take towel baths. They get two washcloths a day. They put soap on one and use it to wash. Then they put water on the other and use it to rinse off the soap.

And how do they wash their hair?

Astronauts use a wet, rinseless shampoo. They gently rub the shampoo into their hair. They try not to make soap bubbles because bubbles are difficult to get out of the air. Then they dry their hair with a towel.

And how do astronauts brush their teeth? They brush their teeth just like they do on earth. Each astronaut has a personal hygiene kit with a toothbrush, toothpaste, and dental floss. The kit also has a comb, a brush, deodorant, and body lotion. There are nail clippers, too. But nails grow very slowly in space, so astronauts cut their nails only once a month.

What do many astronauts miss most about earth? A hot shower!

Astronauts use a rinseless shampoo.

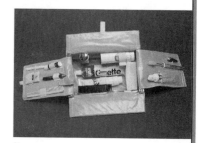
An astronaut's personal hygiene kit.

## ▶ What did you read?

The words in the box make a sentence. Put them in order. Write the sentence on the line.

| keep | ~~Astronauts~~ | space | must | clean | in |

Astronauts _____.

## ▶ Read again

Complete these sentences. Find the answers in the reading. Circle *a* or *b*.
Check your answers with a partner.

1. In space, astronauts must     **a.** get sick.    **(b.)** stay healthy.

2. In space, they can take     **a.** showers.    **b.** towel baths.

3. In space, water floats because it is    **a.** weightless.    **b.** motionless.

4. Astronauts get two washcloths    **a.** a week.    **b.** a day.

5. Their shampoo is    **a.** wet.    **b.** dry.

6. Astronauts cut their nails    **a.** once a week.    **b.** once a month.

## ▶ Write

**A. Circle the questions you want to ask the astronauts. Write two questions of your own.**

1. How long were you in space?
2. What did you like most about space?
3. What did you miss most from earth?
4. _____ ?
5. _____ ?

**B. Write a letter to one of the astronauts on page 34. Copy the letter on your own paper and write in your questions.**

> Dear Astronaut _____,
> I read an article about astronauts. I want to know more about your time in space.
>
> Sincerely,

Write your questions here. —→

Sign your name. —→

## ▶ *Read a graph*

### A. Look at the graph. Answer the questions.

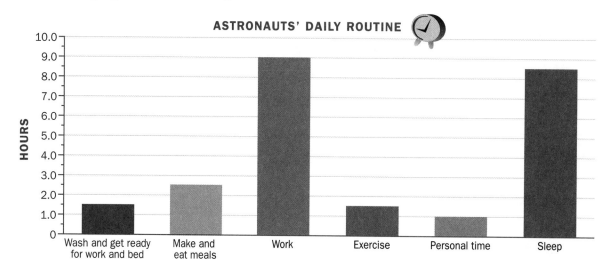

**ASTRONAUTS' DAILY ROUTINE**

1. How long do astronauts sleep?  _8 ½ hours_
2. How long do they take to make and eat their meals?  _____
3. How long do they exercise?  _____
4. How long do they take to wash and get ready for work and bed?  _____
5. How many activities take 1 ½ hours?  _____
6. Which activity takes the most time?  _____

### B. Fill in the graph to show how much time you spend on each activity. Then talk about your answers with a partner.

**YOUR DAILY ROUTINE**

 **Turn to *Remember the Words*, page 105.**

## TALK ABOUT IT

A. Work in a small group. Talk about the kinds of stores you usually go to in a mall or in your community. Write the names of the stores in the correct categories.

**DEPARTMENT STORES**

**CLOTHING STORES**

**SHOE STORES**

**FOOD STORES / RESTAURANTS**

**OTHER STORES**

B. Think about these questions. Then ask and answer the questions with a partner.

1. Where do you like to shop? Downtown? In a mall? In your neighborhood? Why?

2. Which stores are your favorites? Why do you like them?

# READ ABOUT IT

**Mall of America is the largest mall in the U.S.**

## Before You Read

**A.** Look at the pictures and the words under the pictures. Look at the title of the reading. Guess the answer to the question. Circle it.

What is this reading about?

**a.** a different kind of mall      **b.** a day at an amusement park

**B.** Read these sentences. Scan the reading for the answers. Circle them.

1. 90,000 / (900,000) people visit Mall of America each week.

2. 2 / 7 baseball stadiums could fit inside.

3. Mall of America has 9 / 29 shoe stores.

4. It has 22 / 27 fast food restaurants.

5. It cost $130 million / $650 million to build the mall.

6. 10,000 / 100,000 gallons of paint cover the mall.

> scan = look quickly to find specific information

**Read this brochure. Check your answers while you read.**

# MALL OF AMERICA

Do you like to shop? Come to Mall of America in Bloomington, Minnesota. You can be one of the 900,000 shoppers who come to Mall of America every week. Why do so many people shop here? How do so many people fit in the mall? Well, Mall of America is the largest mall in the United States. It is so large, 7 baseball stadiums could fit inside.

People come from all over the world to visit Mall of America. The largest number of international tourists come from Canada, Japan, and the United Kingdom. They come to shop at 500 different stores. There are 6 department stores, 26 women's clothing stores, and 29 shoe stores. There are 4 bookstores, 5 music stores, 6 electronics stores, and many other places to shop.

Are you hungry? Mall of America has 49 restaurants. There are 27 fast food restaurants and 22 sit-down restaurants. What about entertainment? Mall of America has 8 nightclubs and a 14-screen movie theater. You can see fish at an aquarium or play miniature golf. Mall of America also has the world's largest amusement park inside a building—Camp Snoopy. At Camp Snoopy you can even ride an indoor roller coaster!

Mall of America is almost like a small city. It has a bank, a post office, a medical clinic, and a dental clinic. The mall also has 3 schools: a university, an adult school, and a high school. It has hair salons, travel agencies, and florists, too. There is something for everyone at Mall of America!

## MALL FACTS

► *Mall of America opened in 1992.*
► *It cost $650 million to build.*
► *100,000 gallons of paint cover Mall of America.*

See a show at a nightclub.

See fish at the aquarium.

Play miniature golf.

Ride an indoor roller coaster.

## ▶ Read again

**Are these sentences true? Find the answers in the reading. Circle *yes* or *no*. Check your answers with a partner.**

1. Mall of America is the largest mall in the world.          yes          (no)

2. People come from all over the world to visit Mall of America.          yes          no

3. Mall of America has 400 stores.          yes          no

4. The mall has an amusement park and an aquarium.          yes          no

5. You can ride an outdoor roller coaster at the mall.          yes          no

6. The mall has 2 schools.          yes          no

7. You can go to the dentist at the mall.          yes          no

## ▶ Show you understand

**Fill in the blanks with words from the box.**

> movie     restaurants     golf     post office
> ~~large~~     mall     amusement park     city

Mall of America is very _____large_____. It is the largest _____
in the United States. It is like a small _____.
The mall has a bank and a _____. It has many stores and
_____. It has entertainment, too. You can go to
a _____ or play miniature _____.
You can even go to an _____ and ride a roller coaster.

## ▶ Talk more about it

**Think about these questions. Then discuss your ideas.**

> 1. Why do people like to go to malls? Give three reasons.
> 2. Do you want to visit Mall of America? Why or why not?

## After You Read

▶ *Words, words, words*

**Read these sentences. Look at the underlined words. What do they mean?**
**Draw lines to the correct meanings.**

1. What about underlined entertainment?

2. Mall of America has 8 nightclubs.

3. You can see fish at an aquarium.

4. The largest number of international tourists come from Canada, Japan, and the United Kingdom.

5. It is so large, 7 baseball stadiums…

6. …could fit inside.

a. places to eat, drink, dance, and see a show in the evening

b. have enough room

c. something interesting to see or do, for example, a show or a movie

d. a place to see water animals

e. people who travel for fun

f. large places to play and watch sports

▶ *Write*

**Where do you like to shop? What do you usually do on a shopping trip?**
**Write a paragraph about shopping on your own paper. Follow the example.**

I like to shop in my neighborhood. There are many small stores. I usually go to the drugstore and the bookstore. Sometimes I go to the post office to buy stamps. I often stop at the coffee shop for lunch. Before I go home, I always buy a newspaper at the newsstand.

# READ MORE ABOUT IT

## *Before You Read*

**Look at the pictures. Look at the title of the reading. Guess the answers to the questions. Circle them.**

**1**. What is the reading about?

    **a.** teenagers in trouble    **b.** worried adults    **c.** *a* and *b*.

**2.** What are the adults thinking about? Circle the problems you see in the pictures.

    stealing    smoking cigarettes    using illegal drugs    drinking alcohol

          fighting    playing loud music    getting arrested

Read this newspaper article. Think about your guesses while you read.

# Problems in Malls

On Saturdays about 1,500 teenagers go to the Westview Mall in Centerville. Most teens go to shop and meet their friends. A few of them get into trouble. Store owners report many problems. Some teens steal things from stores. Some teens fight or use bad language. Some use illegal drugs or drink alcohol at the mall.

The manager of the mall tried a few things to stop these problems. He added lights in the parking garage. He hired more security guards. He also planned more family activities. But nothing stopped the problems.

Many other malls around the United States are having the same problems with teenagers. Managers at these malls are making rules to stop the problems. Last week the manager of the Westview Mall also made new rules. One new rule says that on weekends kids under 17 must come to the mall with an adult.

A group of parents and church leaders in Centerville are angry. They think the rules are unfair to teenagers. They are scared that police officers will handcuff and arrest their children at the mall. They don't want the teens to go to court because of the new rules.

Now many parents and teenagers will not go to Westview Mall. They are showing the manager they don't like the new rules.

## ▶ Read again

**Are these sentences true? Find the answers in the reading. Circle *yes* or *no*. Check your answers with a partner.**

| | | |
|---|---|---|
| 1. Many teenagers go to malls. | (yes) | no |
| 2. Some teenagers steal at malls. | yes | no |
| 3. Many malls are making rules to stop the problems. | yes | no |
| 4. The new rules say teens can't go to malls. | yes | no |
| 5. All parents think the rules are fair. | yes | no |
| 6. Some teenagers will not go to Westview Mall now. | yes | no |

## ▶ Talk more about it

**Work in a small group. Talk about question 1. Write the problems. Then talk about question 2. Write your solutions. Discuss your ideas with the class.**

**1.** What problems do some teenagers cause at malls?

### Problems

**a.** Some teens steal. _____

**b.** _____

**c.** _____

**d.** _____

**2.** How can the malls stop these problems?

### Solutions

**a.** Hire more security guards. _____

**b.** _____

**c.** _____

**d.** _____

## ▶ Write

**Write a letter to the manager of the Westview Mall or a mall or store near you. Write about one problem and one solution. Copy the letter on your own paper.**

Write the date here.

To the Manager of _____:

Choose one. → Your mall/store has a problem.

The problem is _____.

Here is how you can stop the problem.

_____.

The solution will work because

_____.

Thank you for reading about my ideas.

Sincerely,

Sign your name. →

**Turn to *Remember the Words*, page 105.**

## TALK ABOUT IT

**A. Work with a partner. Quickly list as many different kinds of transportation as you can. Check your answers with another pair of students. Did they list something you did not? Add it to your list.**

| | |
|---|---|
| bus | |
| | |
| | |
| | |

**B. Think about these questions. Then ask and answer the questions with a partner.**

> **1.** How long does it take you to get to school? To work?
> What kind of transportation do you use?
>
> **2.** You are going to a city 250 miles away. How do want to travel?
> By car? By bus? By plane? By train? Why?

# READ ABOUT IT

## Before You Read

**Look at the pictures and the words under the pictures. Look at the title and the subtitles of the reading. Then read the list below and mark (X) the ideas you think will be in the reading.**

_____ Planes will be bigger.　　_____ Planes will be faster.　　_____ Cities will be bigger.

_____ Trains will be bigger.　　_____ Cars will be faster.　　_____ Life will change.

## While You Read

**Read this Web page. Think about your guesses while you read.**

### A NEW WORLD OF TRANSPORTATION

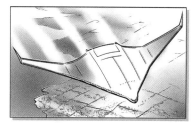
A new large airplane

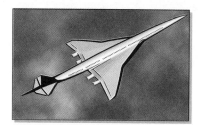
A new high-speed plane

A new high-speed train

Cars and airplanes changed life in the 20th century. New changes in transportation are going to make life very different in the 21st century, too. Trains and planes will be faster and more comfortable. Planes will also be bigger.

#### NEW AIRPLANES

Today the biggest planes carry about 400 passengers. Soon aircraft companies will build larger planes. These new large planes will carry 600–800 passengers.

Now high-speed planes travel from London to New York in 3 hours. They carry only 100 passengers. New high-speed planes will be bigger and faster. They will fly from London to New York in only 1½ hours and they will carry 300 people. A ticket on these fast planes will be very expensive, so most people will not use them.

#### HIGH-SPEED TRAINS

Many people will take new, high-speed trains instead of planes. Today most trains can go 80 miles per hour (130 km/h). Japan's bullet train can go 150 mph (240 km/h). New high-speed trains will go more than 300 mph (480 km/h) — two times faster than the bullet train. Germany, Switzerland, and Japan will be the first countries to use these new high-speed trains. Other countries plan to have the new trains, too. In the future the trains we have today may not be used at all.

#### A NEW WORLD

How will life change with these faster planes and trains? People will be able to live in one city and work in another city. In Switzerland it now takes 3 hours to go from Geneva to Zurich by train. On a new high-speed train the same trip will take only 57 minutes. These fast trains will also make cities grow. More than 100 million people could live in a very large city 125 miles (200 km) wide. On high-speed trains those people could travel from one end of the city to the other in a very short time.

In the 20th century, transportation has changed from horses to cars and from airplanes to high-speed trains and planes. What changes will the 21st century bring?

## ▶ What did you read?

**Choose a different title for this reading. Circle the best one.**

**a.** Life in the 21st Century          **b.** 21st Century Travel

## ▶ Read again

**Choose the right words for these sentences. Find the information in the reading. Circle the correct answers.**

1. High-speed trains and planes changed / will change life in the 21st century.
2. New large planes will carry about 400 / 700 people.
3. Travel on high-speed planes will be expensive / cheap.
4. New high-speed trains will go about 2 times / 4 times faster than most trains today.
5. In the future the trains we have today will / may not be used at all.
6. People will be able to live in one city and sleep / work in another city.

## ▶ Show you understand

**Which kind of transportation is each description about? Mark (X) the correct boxes. Use the reading to help you.**

|  | HIGH-SPEED PLANES | NEW LARGE PLANES | HIGH-SPEED TRAINS |
|---|---|---|---|
| 1. will go from London to New York in 1½ hours | X |  |  |
| 2. will cause cities to grow |  |  |  |
| 3. will carry 600–800 passengers |  |  |  |
| 4. will travel at more than 300 mph |  |  |  |
| 5. will carry 300 passengers |  |  |  |
| 6. will be very expensive for passengers |  |  |  |

## ▶ Talk more about it

**Think about these questions. Then discuss your ideas.**

1. How will most people get to work 20 years from now? By car? By bus? By high-speed train? Why?
2. Are you scared to fly on an airplane, sail on a boat, or go on some other kind of transportation? Why or why not?

## After You Read

▶ *Outline*

**Complete this outline. Find the information in the reading.**

# A New World of Transportation

### I.  *New airplanes*

   A. New large planes will carry _____.

   B. New high-speed planes will be _____ and _____.

   C. A ticket on the high-speed planes will be _____.

### II.  *High-speed trains*

   A. High-speed trains will go _____.

   B. Germany, Switzerland, and Japan will be _____

   _____.

### III.  _____

   A. People will be able _____

   _____.

   B. More than 100,000,000 people could live _____

   _____.

 By the year 2020, planes will carry 1,000–1,400 passengers.

# READ MORE ABOUT IT

## Before You Read

**Look at the picture. Look at the title of the reading. Guess the answers to the questions. Circle them.**

**1.** Where is the man?    **a.** on a plane    **b.** on a bus

**2.** What is the man reading?    **a.** a poem    **b.** an advertisement

## While You Read

**Read this magazine article. Think about your guesses while you read.**

# Poetry in Motion

Do you ride a bus, a subway, or other kind of public transportation? What do you do to pass the time on your way to school, work, or home? Some people read magazines or newspapers. Some people talk or listen to music. In New York, Atlanta, and Chicago many people read poems. People read poems in Portland, Los Angeles, and Dallas, too. They don't bring the poems with them. The poems are on the walls of the buses and subways.

Who puts poems on the walls of public transportation? A group of poets and poetry lovers. They want more people to read poems, so they put them on the buses and subways instead of advertisements. This way many people can read them. They choose poems for people of all ages and from all over the world. They choose poems about traveling on many different kinds of transportation—trains, ferries, and planes. They hope the poems will make the passengers happy and make them think.

Every day 5 million people see the poems in New York City. That is over 1 billion passengers in one year!

Here is one of the poems you may see on a bus or subway. Carl Sandburg, a famous American poet, wrote it.

**Window**
**Night from a railroad car window**
**Is a great, dark, soft thing**
**Broken across with slashes of light.**

## ▶ Read again

**Are these sentences true? Find the answers in the reading. Circle *yes* or *no*. Check your answers with a partner.**

1. Some people read poems on the bus or subway.    (yes)    no

2. A group of passengers puts the poems on the bus.    yes    no

3. The poems are about transportation.    yes    no

4. The poems are only for children.    yes    no

5. In New York 5 billion passengers see the poems every day.    yes    no

6. The poem *Window* is about the night.    yes    no

## ▶ Show you understand

**Read the poem *Window* aloud. Answer the questions. Then discuss your answers with a partner.**

1. What kind of transportation is this poem about? _____

2. Write three words in the poem that describe the night. _____ _____ _____

3. Where do you think the light is coming from? _____

4. How does the poem make you feel? Circle as many words as you want.

     happy     lonely     sad     excited     calm    _____
                                                           (other)

## ▶ Talk more about it

**Think about these questions. Then discuss your ideas.**

1. Is it a good idea to put poems in buses and subways? Why or why not?

2. Do you like poetry? Why or why not?

3. Is poetry popular in your country? Name the most famous poets. Talk about their poetry.

 **Turn to *Remember the Words*, page 105.**

## TALK ABOUT IT

**A. Work with a partner. Read the time line. Are the sentences below true? Circle the answers.**

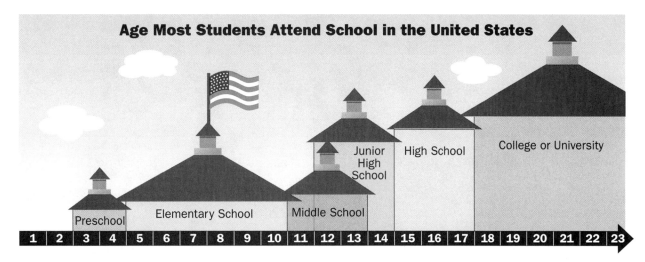

Age Most Students Attend School in the United States

Preschool | Elementary School | Middle School | Junior High School | High School | College or University

1 | 2 | 3 | 4 | 5 | 6 | 7 | 8 | 9 | 10 | 11 | 12 | 13 | 14 | 15 | 16 | 17 | 18 | 19 | 20 | 21 | 22 | 23

1. Many 3-year-olds go to preschool.                          (yes)        no
2. Many young people begin college at 18.                      yes        no
3. Most 13-year-olds go to high school.                        yes        no
4. Many 5-year-olds begin elementary school.                   yes        no
5. A lot of 16-year-olds attend junior high school.            yes        no

**B. Make a time line about schools in your country. Use the time line above as an example. Talk about your time line with your partner.**

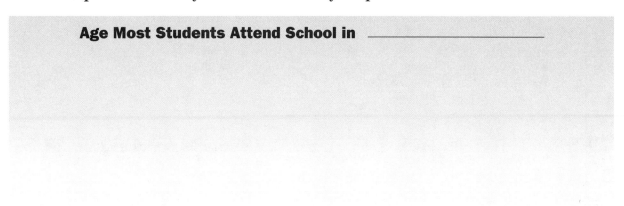

Age Most Students Attend School in _____

1 | 2 | 3 | 4 | 5 | 6 | 7 | 8 | 9 | 10 | 11 | 12 | 13 | 14 | 15 | 16 | 17 | 18 | 19 | 20 | 21 | 22 | 23

## Before You Read

**A. Look at the pictures. Look at the title of the reading. Guess the answers to the questions. Circle them.**

**1.** How old is this boy?

    **a.** 5 years old         **b.** 10 years old       **c.** 18 years old

**2.** Where does he go to school?

    **a.** elementary school    **b.** middle school    **c.** high school    **d.** college

**B. Scan paragraphs 2 and 3. Look for the numbers that show Michael Kearney's age. Match his age to the school he went to then. Work as quickly as you can.**

| Age | School |
| --- | --- |
| 5 years old | high school |
| 6 years old | graduate school |
| 10 years old | community college |
| 12 years old | university |

> scan = look quickly to find specific information

Read this magazine article. Check your answers while you read.

# A *Different* Child

In the United States many children go to preschool at age 3. Most children start elementary school when they are 5 years old. They go to high school at about age 15. When they go to college or vocational school, they usually start at 18. They often graduate from college at the age of 21.    **1**

Michael Kearney is not like most children. He is very, very smart. He began to read when he was 8 months old. At age 3 he read fifth-grade books and began to understand algebra. At age 5 he went to high school. In high school Michael learned very quickly. The classes were too easy for him, and he felt bored. He left high school, and his mother taught him at home.    **2**

When he was 6 years old, he studied at a community college. Then he went to a university. At age 10 he graduated from the university with a Bachelor's degree in anthropology, the study of humans. At the university he also studied about the earth. He took many geography and geology classes. At age 12 he finished graduate school and received his Master's degree in anthropology.    **3**

Michael is still studying. In the future he wants to be the host of a television game show, a college professor, or an actor. Who knows? Michael is very smart, so maybe he will be all three.    **4**

## ▶ Read again

**Read these sentences. Look at the reading to find which sentences are correct. Circle *a* or *b*. Check your answers with a partner.**

1. **a.** In the U.S. many children go to preschool at age 3.
   **b.** In the U.S. many children go to preschool at age 5.

2. **a.** Michael Kearney is like most children.
   **b.** Michael Kearney is not like most children.

3. **a.** At age 3 he read first-grade books.
   **b.** At age 3 he read fifth-grade books.

4. **a.** In high school he felt bored.
   **b.** In high school he felt confused.

5. **a.** Anthropology is the study of the earth.
   **b.** Anthropology is the study of humans.

6. **a.** Michael wants to be a college student.
   **b.** Michael wants to be a college professor.

## ▶ Show you understand

**Fill in the blanks with words from the box.**

| teacher | read | university | home | high school | degree | ~~smart~~ |

Michael Kearney is very _____smart_____. He began to _____

when he was 8 months old. At age 5 he went to _____. It was too easy

for him, so he studied at _____. His mother was his _____.

At age 10 he graduated from a _____. At age 12 he got his

Master's _____.

## ▶ Talk more about it

**Think about these questions. Then discuss your ideas.**

1. Michael started college at 6 years old. What do you think was easy for Michael at college? What was difficult?

2. What do you think will happen to Michael in the future? Will he be smarter than other adults?

3. Some people think 3–5 year old children should play. Some people think they should read, write, and do math. What do you think?

# After You Read

▶ *Skim for the main idea*

**Skim each paragraph in the reading. Draw a line from the paragraph to the main idea.**

skim = read quickly to get the general idea

| Paragraph | Main Idea |
|---|---|
| Paragraph **1** | Michael's college days |
| Paragraph **2** | Michael's future |
| Paragraph **3** | Schooling in the United States |
| Paragraph **4** | Michael's early schooling |

▶ *Words, words, words*

**Read these sentences. Look at the underlined words. What do you think they mean? Circle *a* or *b*.**

1. Most children start elementary school at age 5. They go to high school at about age 15.

   (**a.**) more or less        **b.** less than

2. The high school classes were too easy for Michael. He felt bored.

   **a.** good        **b.** not interested

3. He graduated from the university at age 10 with a Bachelor's degree in anthropology.

   **a.** got good grades at        **b.** finished

4. In the future he wants to be the host of a television game show, ...

   **a.** leader        **b.** player

5. ...a college professor, or an actor.

   **a.** teacher        **b.** student

▶ *Write*

**How is Michael Kearney different from most children in the U.S.? Use *but* to write as many sentences as you can. Follow the examples.**

1. Most children go to preschool at age 3, but Michael read fifth-grade books at age 3.

2. Most children _____, but Michael _____.

3. _____, but _____.

4. _____.

# READ MORE ABOUT IT

## Before You Read

**Look at the pictures and the words under the pictures. Look at the title of the reading. Guess the answers to the questions. Circle them.**

1. Where are the people in the photographs?   **a.** at the circus   **b.** at a school

2. Why are people flying on a trapeze?   **a.** for fun   **b.** for their jobs

## While You Read

**Read this magazine article. Think about your guesses while you read.**

# Circus School

Do you want to fly through the air on a trapeze? Do you want to learn to juggle? Now you don't have to join the circus. You can go to circus school. There are 27 schools around the world—in Canada, England, Australia, and the United States.

Fly through the air on a trapeze.

One of the biggest schools is the San Francisco School of Circus Arts. All kinds of people take classes there. The most popular class is trapeze. On any evening doctors, teachers, hairdressers, and elementary school students line up to fly through the air. The school has students from 4 to 79 years old. Blind and physically challenged students can learn to fly, too. Anyone can do it.

Why do the students do it? "I love the feeling," says a 45-year-old doctor. "When you're at the end of the swing, you're weightless." "I'm scared of high places," says a 17-year-old high school student. "I go on the trapeze to learn not to be scared."

Learn to juggle.

Be careful! When you try it, you may not want to stop. Some of the trapeze teachers first tried it for fun. One man received a Bachelor's degree in economics. Then he tried trapeze. Now he teaches trapeze, not economics! Another teacher was a college student when she first tried it. She says, "I didn't finish college. I ran away and joined the circus."

## ▶ Read again

**Are these sentences true? Find the answers in the reading. Circle _yes_ or _no_.**
**Then check your answers with a partner.**

1. All kinds of people take trapeze classes.    (yes)    no

2. You can learn trapeze and juggling at
   elementary school.    yes    no

3. Five-year-old children can learn trapeze at the
   San Francisco school.    yes    no

4. You must join the circus to take trapeze classes.    yes    no

5. People who try trapeze usually like it.    yes    no


## ▶ Words, words, words

**Read these sentences. Look at the <u>underlined</u> words. What do they mean?**
**Draw lines to the correct meanings.**

1. Trapeze is the <u>most popular</u> class
   at the school.

2. ...students <u>line up</u> to fly through the air.

3. One man <u>received</u> a Bachelor's degree
   in economics.

4. I <u>ran away</u> and joined the circus.

**a.** got

**b.** left home and
did not tell anyone

**c.** favorite

**d.** wait their turn


## ▶ Talk more about it

**Think about these questions. Then discuss your ideas.**

1. Why do all kinds of people like trapeze?

2. Do you want to take trapeze classes? Why or why not?

## ▶ *Write and read*

**A. What kinds of classes does your community offer? Choose a class in your community or from the brochure below. Write a paragraph about the class on your own paper. Tell why you want to take it. Follow the example.**

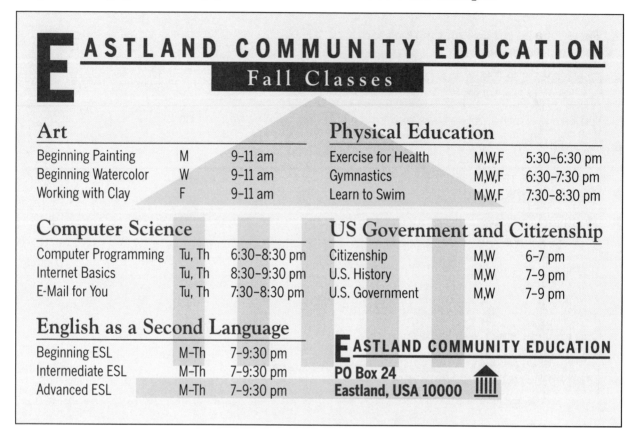

**EASTLAND COMMUNITY EDUCATION**

**Fall Classes**

### Art

| | | |
|---|---|---|
| Beginning Painting | M | 9–11 am |
| Beginning Watercolor | W | 9–11 am |
| Working with Clay | F | 9–11 am |

### Computer Science

| | | |
|---|---|---|
| Computer Programming | Tu, Th | 6:30–8:30 pm |
| Internet Basics | Tu, Th | 8:30–9:30 pm |
| E-Mail for You | Tu, Th | 7:30–8:30 pm |

### English as a Second Language

| | | |
|---|---|---|
| Beginning ESL | M–Th | 7–9:30 pm |
| Intermediate ESL | M–Th | 7–9:30 pm |
| Advanced ESL | M–Th | 7–9:30 pm |

### Physical Education

| | | |
|---|---|---|
| Exercise for Health | M,W,F | 5:30–6:30 pm |
| Gymnastics | M,W,F | 6:30–7:30 pm |
| Learn to Swim | M,W,F | 7:30–8:30 pm |

### US Government and Citizenship

| | | |
|---|---|---|
| Citizenship | M,W | 6–7 pm |
| U.S. History | M,W | 7–9 pm |
| U.S. Government | M,W | 7–9 pm |

**EASTLAND COMMUNITY EDUCATION**

**PO Box 24**
**Eastland, USA 10000**

I want to take Beginning Painting. I like painting very much. I want to have fun and learn about art. I also want to paint pictures for my home.

**B. Find a partner. Read your partner's paragraph. Write the name of the class he or she chose below. Do the same with three more partners.**

1. _____

2. _____

3. _____

4. _____

 **Turn to *Remember the Words*, page 105.**

## TALK ABOUT IT

**A. Work in a small group. Look at the picture. Write the names of the animals you know in the correct boxes.**

| LAND ANIMALS | SEA ANIMALS | BIRDS | INSECTS |
| --- | --- | --- | --- |
| | dolphin | | |

**B. Think about these questions. Then ask and answer the questions with a partner.**

1. Which animal is your favorite? Why? Give three reasons.

2. Which animals do you think can talk or communicate in some way with humans? Name three animals.

**Dr. Penny Patterson taught Koko
to use American Sign Language.**

**Dr. Irene Pepperberg
taught Alex to talk.**

## Before You Read

**Look at the pictures and the words near the pictures. Guess the answers
and fill in the blanks.**

**1.** Alex is a _____ .
(animal)

**2.** He speaks _____ .
(language)

**3.** Koko is a _____ .
(animal)

**4.** She uses _____ .
(language)

Do you want to read "Alex" (page 65) or "Koko" (page 66)?
Choose one article to read. Don't read the other one yet.

## *While You Read*

**Read this magazine article. Think about your guesses while you read.**

# Alex

Are animals like humans? Do they have feelings? Can they talk? Some people are studying animals. They are finding out many interesting things.

Dr. Irene Pepperberg is a scientist at the University of Arizona. She is studying parrots. She wants to find out how their brains work. She taught an African gray parrot to speak English. His name is Alex. He can say more than 100 English words! He also understands them.

Dr. Pepperberg asks Alex questions, and he answers in English. In this way, she knows what Alex's brain can do. Alex can name forty objects. He can also name five shapes, four materials, and seven colors. He can solve problems and answer questions. He gives the correct answer

80% of the time. For example, Dr. Pepperberg shows Alex a tray with objects on it—blue metal cubes, green balls made of wood, and red plastic squares. Alex looks at the objects.

Dr. Pepperberg: "Which shape is plastic?"
Alex: *"Square!"*
Dr. Pepperberg: "Good birdie!"
Alex: *"Can I have a nut?"*
Dr. Pepperberg: "All right, you can have a nut."

Most people think animals are very different from humans. Dr. Pepperberg learned that Alex can do some of the same things humans can do. Animals are more like humans than we think. ■

Now do the exercises on page 67.

## *While You Read*

**Read this magazine article. Think about your guesses while you read.**

# Koko

**Are animals like humans? Do they have feelings? Can they talk? Some people are studying animals. They are finding out many interesting things.**

Dr. Penny Patterson is a psychologist. She started the Gorilla Foundation of California. She studies the way animals and humans do things. She wants to know if gorillas are like humans. Can they talk? Can they use tools? Dr. Patterson is studying Koko, a 230-pound lowland gorilla. Koko can't speak, but she talks with her hands. She uses American Sign Language, or ASL. ASL is the hand language of the deaf. Dr. Patterson taught Koko more than 1000 signs.

Koko is very smart. She is almost as smart as a human child. Koko can ask and answer questions. She talks about the past and the future. She can also use a computer and a camera. Dr. Patterson wants to know if gorillas have feelings. Koko does! She tells Dr. Patterson when she feels happy or sad. One day Koko did something bad. Dr. Patterson talked to Koko about it in ASL.

Dr. Patterson: "What did you do to Penny?"
Koko: *"Bite. Sorry bite."*
Dr. Patterson: "Why bite?"
Koko: *"Because mad."*
Dr. Patterson: "Why mad?"
Koko: *"Don't know."*

Most people think animals are very different from humans. Dr. Patterson learned that Koko can do some of the same things humans can do. Animals are more like humans than we think. ■

Now do the exercises on page 67.

## ▶ Read again

**A. Work with a partner who chose the same reading. Answer the questions in the chart. Write your answers in the column that goes with your reading.**

|  | ALEX | KOKO |
|---|---|---|
| **1.** What kind of animal did you read about? | | |
| **2.** What language does the animal use? | | |
| **3.** How many words/signs does the animal know? | | |
| **4.** Who taught the animal the language? Why? | | |
| **5.** What can the animal do? | | |

**B. With your partner, find a pair of students who chose the other reading. Ask them the questions in the chart and write their answers.**

## ▶ Read more

Did you read about Alex? Now read about Koko on page 66.
Did you read about Koko? Now read about Alex on page 65.

## ▶ Talk more about it

**Think about these questions. Then discuss your ideas.**

1. Who is smarter, Alex or Koko? Why do you think so?

2. Do animals have feelings? Talk about Alex, Koko, or an animal you know.

3. What other animals do you think scientists study? Why?

## After You Read

▶ *Pronouns*

**Look at the circled words. What do they mean? Draw an arrow to the words that tell the meaning.**

1. Are animals like humans? Do (they) have feelings?

2. Dr. Irene Pepperberg is a scientist at the University of Arizona. (She) is studying parrots.

3. Dr. Pepperberg asks Alex questions, and (he) answers in English.

4. For example, Dr. Pepperberg shows Alex a tray with objects on (it).

5. Dr. Patterson wants to know if gorillas are like humans. Can (they) talk?

▶ *Write*

**Write sentences about Alex and Koko. Use the readings to help you. Follow the examples.**

1. How are Alex and Koko alike?

   Alex and Koko both answer questions.

   _____

   _____

   _____

   _____

   _____

2. How are Alex and Koko different?

   Alex lives in Arizona, but Koko lives in California.

   _____

   _____

   _____

   _____

   _____

# READ MORE ABOUT IT

## Before You Read

Look at the picture and the words under the picture. Look at the title
of the reading. Guess the answers to the questions.

1. What is the gorilla doing? _____

2. What is going to happen next? _____

## While You Read

Read this newspaper article. Think about your guesses while you read.

# Gorilla Saves Boy

**Gorilla hero, Binti Jua**

Binti Jua and her baby, Koola, are gorillas. They live with five other gorillas in the Brookfield Zoo near Chicago. Many people come to see them because they are so big and strong.

On August 16, 1996 a large crowd of people was watching the gorillas. A three-year-old boy was watching them, too. He was excited to see the gorillas. He was so excited, he walked away from his mother. Then he climbed on the rocks that keep the gorillas from getting out. Suddenly he fell 18 feet (6 m) and landed near the gorillas. The boy hit his head and was knocked unconscious. He didn't move.

The people were worried. How could they save the boy? It was too dangerous to go near the gorillas to get him.

Binti got up and went over to the boy. What would she do? Would she hurt the boy? She touched him, but he didn't move. Binti knew something was wrong with the boy. She picked him up. The boy's mother was scared. She cried, "The gorilla has my baby!" But Binti gently carried him and put him down near the door. A zookeeper opened the door and took the boy out.

Everyone cheered. They were surprised and relieved. Binti saved the boy!

The boy is OK now, and Binti is a hero. Thousands of people line up to see her every day at the zoo.

## ▶ Read again

**Are these sentences true? Find the answers in the reading. Circle *yes* or *no*.
Check your answers with a partner.**

1. A boy fell off the rocks and landed near the gorillas.  (yes)  no
2. The people watching helped the boy.  yes  no
3. Binti helped the boy.  yes  no
4. A zookeeper helped the boy.  yes  no
5. Many people come to see Binti because she is a hero.  yes  no

## ▶ Talk more about it

**Think about these questions. Then discuss your ideas.**

1. Why do you think Binti saved the boy? Give two reasons.
2. How do animals help people? Name three ways.

## ▶ Puzzle

**Read the sentences below. Find the words in the box that go in each sentence.
Write the words in the puzzle. Follow the example.**

~~climbed~~   dangerous   landed   cheered   gently   wrong   hero

**Down**

1. A boy was so excited, he ____ on the rocks.
2. The boy is OK now and Binti is a ____.
3. It was too ____ to go near the gorillas to get the boy.

**Across**

1. Everyone ____. They were surprised and relieved.
4. Suddenly he fell and ____ near the gorillas.
5. She picked him up and ____ carried him to the door.
6. Binti knew something was ____ with the boy.

 **Turn to *Remember the Words*, page 105.**

## TALK ABOUT IT

**A. Work with a partner. Draw lines from the interests to the occupations that match. You can add two interests of your own.**

**Interests**

*You like to:*

read

be outdoors

work with your hands

be with other people

work with math

work with computers

help people

_____

_____

**Occupations**

*So you might like to be:*

an engineer

a police officer

a teacher

a computer programmer

an auto mechanic

an accountant

an assembler

a doctor/nurse

a construction worker

a gardener

**B. How do you find an occupation you like? Start by thinking about these questions. Then talk about your answers with your partner.**

**1.** What are your interests? What do you like to do best? Name as many things as you can.

**2.** Choose one thing you like to do. Which occupations match? Name as many as you can.

# READ ABOUT IT

## Before You Read

Look at the pictures. Look at the title of the reading. Guess the answers
to the questions. Circle them.

1. Who is the young woman talking to in picture 1?  **a.** a teacher  **b.** a counselor

2. Who is the young woman talking to in picture 2?  **a.** a teenager  **b.** a parent

## While You Read

Read this newspaper article. Think about your guesses while you read.

## How to Find an Occupation You Love

Ming Chen wanted to find an occupation, so she went to see Mr. DaCosta. Mr. DaCosta is a counselor at Ming's school. "What do you like to do?" he asked. "I don't know," Ming said. "Well, I like to talk to my friends. Is there a job where I can talk to people?"

Mr. DaCosta asked Ming to make a list. "Write down occupations where people talk to other people," he said. Ming wrote down *salesperson*, *nurse*, *receptionist*, *teacher*, *police officer*, *counselor*, and *lawyer*.

Mr. DaCosta asked Ming to choose the occupation she liked best. She chose counselor. Then he asked her to find the names of places where counselors work. He told her to look at the job board at the employment office. He also told her to look in the classifieds and the telephone book.

Ming found many places where counselors work. The place she liked best was the Teen Counseling Center. She called the Center to ask for information and talked to Ms. Wolff, one of the teen counselors. Ms. Wolff's job was interesting. Part of her job was to talk to teens with problems. She also looked for teen volunteers. Ms. Wolff asked Ming to be a volunteer. Ming wanted to try it. She took a training class and learned how to listen. After the training Ming was a volunteer at the Center three days a week. She listened to teens talk about their problems on the telephone. Ming didn't get paid, but she loved the job. She got a lot of work experience, too.

After six months the Teen Counseling Center hired Ming for the summer. They gave her

a good salary. Now she wants to go to college to get a degree in counseling. She already filled out applications to a few colleges. Ming is lucky. She found an occupation she loves.

## ▶ Read again

**Read these sentences. Look at the reading to find which sentence is correct. Circle *a* or *b*. Check your answers with a partner.**

1. **(a.)** Ming wanted to find an occupation.　　**b.** Ming wanted to find a friend.

2. **a.** She made a list of jobs where people help other people.　　**b.** She made a list of jobs where people talk to other people.

3. **a.** She called the Teen Counseling Center for information.　　**b.** She called the Teen Counseling Center for help.

4. **a.** First Ming got paid at the Teen Counseling Center.　　**b.** First Ming was a volunteer at the Teen Counseling Center.

5. **a.** During the summer she was a volunteer.　　**b.** During the summer she got paid.

6. **a.** Now Ming wants to be a teacher.　　**b.** Now Ming wants to be a counselor.

## ▶ Show you understand

**How did Ming get a job at the Teen Counseling Center? Put the sentences in order to show the steps Ming took.**

__1__ She thought about what she liked to do.

_____ She chose one place she liked.

_____ She chose one occupation.

_____ She made a list of occupations that matched what she liked to do.

_____ She looked for the names of places where people work in that occupation.

_____ She volunteered to work there.

_____ She called and talked to someone who worked at that place.

## ▶ Talk more about it

**Think about these questions. Then discuss your ideas.**

> 1. Why did Ming volunteer at the Teen Counseling Center? What did she learn as a volunteer? Did you ever volunteer? What did you do?
>
> 2. Do you work outside or inside the home? What do you like about your work? What don't you like about it?

## After You Read

▶ *Words, words, words*

**Read these sentences. Look at the <u>underlined</u> words. What do they mean? Draw lines to the correct meanings.**

1. Ming wanted to find an <u>occupation</u>.
2. Mr. DaCosta is a <u>counselor</u> at Ming's school.
3. He told her to look at the job board at the <u>employment office</u>.
4. Ms. Wolff asked Ming to be a <u>volunteer</u>.
5. Ming took a <u>training class</u>.

  **a.** person who works for no pay
  **b.** class to teach a person how to do something
  **c.** job or profession
  **d.** place that helps you find a job
  **e.** person who helps with problems

▶ *Write*

**Think about a job or occupation you want to have in the future. What do you want to do? Where will you work? What will you do every day? Write a paragraph about the occupation on your own paper. Follow the example.**

I want to be an accountant. I will work at an office near my house. I will use a calculator and a computer. I will keep the books for my customers.

# READ MORE ABOUT IT

## Before You Read

**Look at the picture. Look at the title of the reading. Guess the answer to the question.**

How is this company different from other companies you know about?

---

## While You Read

**Read this magazine article. Think about your guess while you read.**

### DREAM BENEFITS

Close your eyes and think about a wonderful place to work. See a beautiful office building with large windows in the middle of a park. Gardeners are planting flowers and mowing the lawn in front of a childcare center. Construction workers are finishing a medical clinic. See yourself working for this company.

Before work you leave your children at the childcare center. Caregivers watch them during the day. At break time you visit your children or take a walk in the park. At noon you and your children have an inexpensive lunch in the cafeteria. Company cooks make delicious, healthy food. During lunch musicians play beautiful music. After work you exercise in the health club in your building.

You have good health insurance. When your children get sick, they can see a doctor at the new medical clinic. When you have a toothache, you can visit a dentist there, too.

Is this a dream? No! More and more companies are giving their employees benefits like these. These benefits save employees' time. They save the company's money. The benefits help workers have a good life. People work hard for a company that helps them be happy and healthy.

## ▶ *What did you read?*

**The words in the box make a sentence about the reading. Put them in order.
Write the sentence on the line.**

| happy | ~~A~~ | worker | a | does | job | good |

A _____.

## ▶ *Read again*

**List the benefits the company gives workers in the first column of this chart. Then
mark (X) how each benefit helps workers. Talk about your answers with a partner.**

| BENEFIT | SAVES TIME | SAVES MONEY | KEEPS WORKERS HEALTHY | KEEPS WORKERS HAPPY |
|---|---|---|---|---|
| 1. childcare center | X | X | | X |
| 2. | | | | |
| 3. | | | | |
| 4. | | | | |
| 5. | | | | |

## ▶ *Write*

**Look at the benefits below. Circle three that are important to you. Use them
to complete the sentences below. Then talk about your sentences with a partner.**

| health insurance | (health club) | a medical clinic |
| a childcare center | a company cafeteria |

1. _____A health club_____ is important because _____I like to exercise_____.
2. _____ is important because _____.
3. _____ is _____.
4. _____.

 **Turn to *Remember the Words*, page 105.**

## TALK ABOUT IT

**A. Look at the pictures. Read the list of sports below. Add a sport of your own. Mark each sport with ✗, ✓, or +. You can mark the sports more than once.**

> ✗ = sports you played when you were younger
> ✓ = sports you play now
> + = sports you want to play in the future

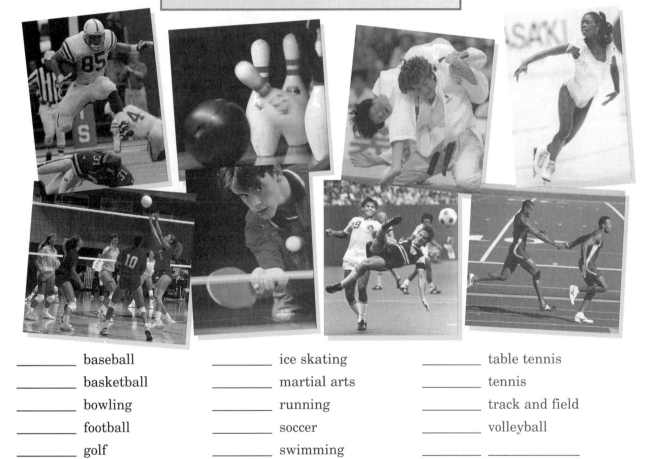

| | | |
|---|---|---|
| _____ baseball | _____ ice skating | _____ table tennis |
| _____ basketball | _____ martial arts | _____ tennis |
| _____ bowling | _____ running | _____ track and field |
| _____ football | _____ soccer | _____ volleyball |
| _____ golf | _____ swimming | _____ _____ |

**B. Ask and answer these questions with a partner.**

1. What sports did you play when you were younger?
2. What sports do you play now or want to play in the future?
3. What is your favorite sport? Why? Give two reasons.

### "I decided to be the greatest athlete that ever lived."

Babe led her team to win a national basketball championship.

Babe was good at track and field.

Babe won three Olympic track and field events.

Babe won 31 professional golf tournaments.

---

### *Before You Read*

Look at the pictures and the words under the pictures. Guess the answer to the question. Circle it.

What was special about Babe Didrikson Zaharias?

**a.** Babe played many sports.　　**c.** Babe was a professional athlete.

**b.** Babe won many tournaments.　**d.** *a*, *b*, and *c*.

---

Do you want to read "Babe's Early Life" (page 79) or "Babe's Dream Comes True" (page 80)? Choose one article to read. Don't read the other one yet.

## While You Read

**Read this textbook page. Think about your guess while you read.**

# Babe's Early Life

Today many women are athletes. They compete in the Olympics and they play professional sports, too. That was not true many years ago. People thought women were too weak to play sports. They thought women might get hurt when they ran or jumped. Some women thought this idea was wrong. They worked hard to become athletes. One of the first professional women athletes was Babe Didrikson Zaharias.

Babe was born in 1911. Her real name was Mildred, but the kids in the neighborhood called her Babe. She could hit home runs just like Babe Ruth, the best baseball player at that time. She could also kick a football very far—farther than any of the boys in the neighborhood. She could play basketball, too. She was the best player on her high school basketball team. Once Babe scored 104 points in one game. She was also on the baseball, volleyball, swimming, and tennis teams at her high school. Babe loved sports.

After high school Babe began to do track and field. She went to her first track meet in 1930. She competed in four events and won all of them.

In the same year a company hired Babe to work as a secretary and play basketball on the company team. She played well and led her team to win a national basketball championship in 1931. Babe was an incredible athlete.

---

## ▶ Read again

**Are these sentences true? Find the answers in the reading. Circle *yes* or *no*. Check your answers with a partner who chose the same reading.**

| | | |
|---|---|---|
| **1.** Babe's friends called her Mildred. | yes | (no) |
| **2.** She was good at many sports. | yes | no |
| **3.** She was the best player on her high school basketball team. | yes | no |
| **4.** She played only one sport in high school. | yes | no |
| **5.** She was good at track and field. | yes | no |
| **6.** She led her team to win a national baseball championship. | yes | no |

Now do the exercises on page 81.

**Read this textbook page. Think about your guess while you read.**

## Babe's Dream Comes True

Today many women are athletes. They compete in the Olympics and they play professional sports, too. That was not true many years ago. People thought women were too weak to play sports. They thought women might get hurt when they ran or jumped. Some women thought this idea was wrong. They worked hard to become athletes. One of the first professional women athletes was Babe Didrikson Zaharias.

When Babe was a teenager, she had a dream. She wanted to be a great athlete. In 1930 at age 19, Babe began to do track and field. In 1932 she competed in a national track and field meet. Babe won first place in five events and tied for first place in another event—all in three hours!

Two weeks later Babe went to the Olympics. She competed in three events and won medals in all three. She was the only person to win running, throwing, *and* jumping events.

After the Olympics Babe was famous. Everybody knew about Babe. She began to play many different sports—bowling, billiards, tennis, and baseball. She also played professional basketball. Then she started to play golf. In 1946 she won 17 golf tournaments in a row.

In 1949 Babe helped start the Ladies Professional Golf Association (LPGA). She later won 31 LPGA tournaments. In 1950 the newspapers called her the "greatest female athlete." Her dream came true!

### ▶ *Read again*

**Complete these sentences. Find the answers in the reading. Circle *a* or *b*. Check your answers with a partner who chose the same reading.**

1. Babe wanted to be a     **a.** great actor.    **b.** great athlete.
2. In a national track and field meet, she won     **a.** three events.    **b.** five events.
3. In the Olympics she won     **a.** two medals.    **b.** three medals.
4. After the Olympics she played     **a.** many sports.    **b.** one sport.
5. In the LPGA she played     **a.** billiards.    **b.** golf.
6. She won     **a.** 17 LPGA tournaments.    **b.** 31 LPGA tournaments.

Now do the exercises on page 81.

▶ *Show you understand*

**A.** Look at the time line with your partner.
Read the sentences under the title of the article
you read. Scan the article for the year that matches
each sentence.

scan = look quickly to find
specific information

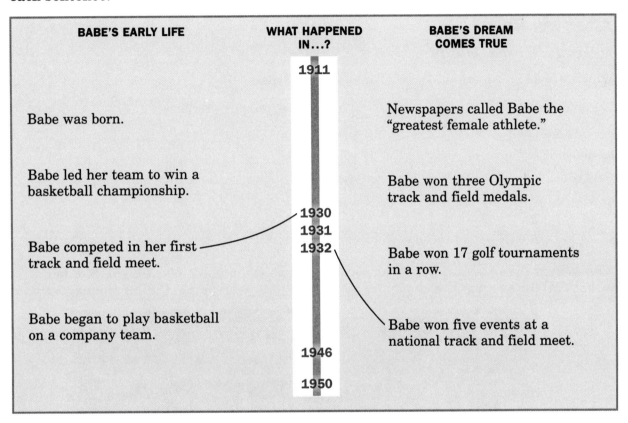

| BABE'S EARLY LIFE | WHAT HAPPENED IN...? | BABE'S DREAM COMES TRUE |
|---|---|---|
| | 1911 | |
| Babe was born. | | Newspapers called Babe the "greatest female athlete." |
| Babe led her team to win a basketball championship. | | Babe won three Olympic track and field medals. |
| | 1930 | |
| | 1931 | |
| Babe competed in her first track and field meet. | 1932 | Babe won 17 golf tournaments in a row. |
| Babe began to play basketball on a company team. | | Babe won five events at a national track and field meet. |
| | 1946 | |
| | 1950 | |

**B.** With your partner, find a pair of students who chose the other reading.
Ask them questions to complete the time line.

Example: *What happened in 1930?*
*Babe competed in her first track and field meet.*

▶ *Talk more about it*

**Think about these questions. Then discuss your ideas.**

1. Who are some professional women athletes? What sports do
they play?

2. What makes one person become a great athlete? Talk about Babe
as one example.

3. Who is a famous athlete in your country? Why is he or she famous?

► ***Read more***

> Did you read "Babe's Early Life"? Now read "Babe's Dream Comes True" on page 80.
> Did you read "Babe's Dream Comes True"? Now read "Babe's Early Life" on page 79.

## After You Read

► ***Words, words, words***

**Which words go together? Draw a line to match them.**

1. game                        **a.** running, jumping, throwing

2. track and field           **b.** player

3. tournament               **c.** event

4. play                         **d.** meet

5. athlete                   **e.** compete

► ***Write***

**Who is your favorite athlete? What sport does she or he play? Why do you like her or him? Write a paragraph about the athlete on your own paper. Follow the example.**

Jackie Joyner-Kersee is my favorite athlete. She won six Olympic medals in track and field. She also plays basketball. I like her because she is fast and strong. She is one of the world's greatest athletes.

# READ MORE ABOUT IT

## Before You Read

**Look at the picture. Look at the title of the reading. Guess the answers to the questions.**

1. What sport are these people watching?   **a.** soccer   **b.** basketball

2. Fans are people who   **a.** are good at sports.   **b.** like sports.

## While You Read

**Read this magazine article. Think about your guesses while you read.**

# TV Sports Fans

All over the world, sports fans cheer when they watch their favorite athletes on television. About 3.5 billion people watch the Olympics. More than 2 billion soccer fans watch the World Cup and 750 million football fans watch the Super Bowl.

Fans from 180 countries watch soccer, the most popular sport in the world. In Italy everything stops when their soccer team is on TV. The same thing happens in Brazil and other countries. In their homes and outside, people get together to watch their team on TV. When their team scores a goal, the shouts of the fans fill the streets.

In 1992 basketball fans around the world saw the "Dream Team," the U.S. Olympic Basketball Team, on TV. Everyone was excited when the "Dream Team" won the gold medal. After the Olympics more people began to watch the National Basketball Association (NBA) games on TV. In Asia the number of TV basketball fans is growing faster than in any other place. About 250 million Chinese can watch NBA games every week. People in Japan, Taiwan, and South Korea are now big NBA basketball fans, too.

In the United States fans watch TV sports programs every day of the week. They watch all kinds of sports—from ice skating to tennis, from martial arts to volleyball. Many Americans celebrate holidays by watching their favorite sports on TV. On Thanksgiving there are two professional football games to watch. There are usually five college football games on New Year's Day. Fans often have parties to watch the big football, baseball, and basketball games with their friends and families.

For the fans, sports are entertainment. Sports bring excitement to their lives. When their team wins, the fans feel like winners, too.●

## ▶ *Read again*

**Are these sentences true? Find the answers in the reading. Circle *yes* or *no*.**

1. About 3.5 billion people watch the World Cup.      yes      (no)
2. Basketball is the most popular sport in the world.      yes      no
3. Soccer is important to people in Italy and Brazil.      yes      no
4. In Asia many people watch basketball on TV.      yes      no
5. On some holidays American fans watch football.      yes      no
6. Fans think it's fun to watch TV sports.      yes      no

## ▶ *Show you understand*

**Fill in the blanks with words from the box.**

| team | ~~sports~~ | cheer | wins | popular | fans |
|------|--------|-------|------|---------|------|

People like to watch _____*sports*_____ on TV. The most _____

sport in the world is soccer. _____ get together in their homes and

outside to watch their _____ play. The fans _____ and

shout when their team scores. When their team _____ , they celebrate.

## ▶ *Talk more about it*

**Think about these questions. Then discuss your ideas.**

1. Why do people like to watch sports on TV? Give three reasons.
2. Which sports do you watch on TV? How many hours a week do you watch?
3. What are the most popular sports in your country? Why do people like them?

 **Turn to *Remember the Words*, page 105.**

# TEACHER'S NOTES

## Teaching the Units

There are three main sections in each unit. TALK ABOUT IT introduces the topic and activates students' prior knowledge. READ ABOUT IT and READ MORE ABOUT IT each contain the components of an effective reading lesson: pre-reading, reading, and post-reading activities.

### Before You Read

Teachers can make these pre-reading activities most effective by initially leading the students through them, thereby modeling the strategies a competent reader uses prior to reading a text. The strategies are repeated and reinforced as students progress through the book.

New vocabulary is most effectively presented in context. In *Read All About It 1*, many new vocabulary words are evident in the picture captions or the *Before You Read* questions. To help students guess the meaning of the words, the teacher can point out any clues in the captions, questions, or pictures that may inform the students' guessing. Modeling this approach to guessing meaning from context is an effective way to accustom students to using the strategy themselves. To avoid overwhelming the students, working with a maximum of about eight new words is recommended.

New words are often reviewed in the *After You Read* section of each unit. When students encounter words they want to learn they can record them in their personal vocabulary diary, Remember the Words on page 105.

Each reading incorporates a number of words from the corresponding unit and other units of *The Oxford Picture Dictionary*, so the readings can be used to reinforce that vocabulary. See page 96 for the Word List with references to *The Oxford Picture Dictionary*.

### While You Read

Since reading is most often a solitary activity, silent reading is an important part of the learning process. Therefore, the readings in this text, with the exception of the poems, are meant to be read individually and silently first. Once students have worked thoroughly with the reading and follow-up exercises, the teacher or students may read the passage aloud to work on pronunciation and to develop fluency in oral reading. The accompanying audio tape can also be used at this time.

Students should be encouraged to guess the meaning of unknown words from context or skip over them just as competent readers do. Teachers should point out to students that they will usually be able to grasp the main ideas of the readings and answer the comprehension questions without understanding every word. They should read for general meaning the first time and refer back to the reading for details during the *Read again* exercises.

The teacher may want to set a short time limit for students to read the passage in the *While You Read* section, and to answer the questions in *What did you read?* and *Read again*. A time limit encourages students to rely on context clues for meaning. It also allows all the students to finish reading and answering the first set of questions simultaneously, so that they can begin pair or group work at the same time.

Although reading the passage and doing the *Read again* exercises are intended to be done individually, the rest of the activities in *While You Read* are designed for pairs or small groups. Working together gives students the opportunity to negotiate the meaning of the readings and to develop communication skills. During group work, it is helpful to give students a time limit to complete the work and to assign student roles, such as discussion leader, recorder, reporter, or timekeeper to help the groups run smoothly. Frequently changing pairings or groupings gives students the experience of listening and talking to a variety of speakers.

While communication skills are an important part of the learning process, all exercises can be completed individually if necessary, and most answers can be found in the Answer Key starting on page 91.

### After You Read

In this section reading skills are reinforced through vocabulary and writing activities. These activities can be done individually in class or used for homework or assessment purposes.

### READ MORE ABOUT IT

Since READ MORE ABOUT IT will probably take place in a new class period, teachers may want to conduct a review discussion of the topic. They can rely on students who read the first passage for answers to specific review questions. More general questions can be answered by those who did not read the first passage. In this way, all students can benefit from the discussion.

## Time Frame

*Read All About It 1* is easily adaptable to different class situations. Activities can be done in a relatively short period of time or exploited to the fullest extent, depending on the needs and goals of the students and the time available. In a TALK ABOUT IT section, for example, a teacher could lead students through the activities to shorten the time or have them work in small groups to lengthen it. Teachers can omit activities that do not suit their objectives.

Units can be easily divided to span more than one class period. In one class, students can complete TALK ABOUT IT through *Talk more about it* for the first reading. *After You Read* can be done for homework. READ MORE ABOUT IT can be reserved for another class period.

## Unit-by-Unit Notes

The following notes provide information and ideas for both new and experienced teachers.

**Procedural Notes (PRO)** offer ideas for specific lesson plans and classroom management.

**Extension Activities (EXT)** are additional reading, writing, or discussion tasks in which students can apply the skills they have learned.

**Word Families (WF)** identify important relationships among word meaning, form, and use. Have students scan the reading for the words and read the sentences where they find them. Then have them use the words in oral or written sentences.

**References (REF)** list sources of further information for students and teachers. Please note that Internet addresses may change.

## Unit 1  Money Troubles

### *The Smell of Bread*

**Page 2, While You Read**

**WF:** *v.* smell   *n.* smell   *v.* smelling

**Page 3, Show you understand**

**EXT:** Students copy the sentences in order to make a paragraph. Those who need a challenge can add other details they remember.

### *You Are a Winner!*

**Page 5, While You Read**

**EXT:** It is common for people to be cheated by mail or telephone solicitations. Older people, immigrants, and foreign students are especially susceptible. Have students brainstorm a list of ways to avoid being cheated, e.g. Never pay money to collect a prize.

**EXT:** Have students change all the numerals they find in the story to the written forms, e.g. *1* to *one*.

**WF:** *v.* costs   *n.* cost   *v.* win   *n.* winner

## Unit 2 Seeing Double

### Page 7, Talk About It

**EXT:** Have students ask each other: Do you know any twins? Do they look the same or different? How do they feel about being twins?

### *Two of a Kind*

**Page 9, Talk more about it**

**EXT:** People often stare at the Rickets twins. Have students talk about staring in their home countries. Is it polite? Why or why not?

### Page 10, Skim for the topic

**PRO:** Model the activity. Write the four topics on the board, explaining that each one tells the main idea of a paragraph in the reading. Elicit words that students might encounter in a paragraph about Hobbies and Activities and write them on the board. Do the same for Physical Description. Give the students about 30 seconds to skim paragraph 1 for words that are frequently repeated and ask them to choose the correct topic. Have them complete the exercise on their own.

**Page 10, Extra! Extra!**

**REF:** http://www.twinsdays.org/

### A Double Wedding

**Page 12, Talk more about it**

Ann Landers, in her advice column, often includes "how we met" stories where people tell how they met their spouses. This reading is based on one such story in which Ann writes about herself.

**EXT:**

1. Ask students: How do you think Ann told the law student she wouldn't marry him? In a letter? In person? How would you tell someone?
2. Have students write a "how we met" story about one of these topics: a. Tell how you met your boyfriend/girlfriend or husband/wife. b. Tell how your parents or other family members or friends met. c. Tell how you think you will meet your future boyfriend/girlfriend or husband/wife.
3. Have students read and discuss other Ann Landers "how we met" columns.

**REF:**
http://www.creators.com/lifestyle/landers/lan.asp

## Unit 3 Home Sweet Home

### Sarah Winchester and the Mystery House

The Winchester Rifle Company made a fortune selling guns. During the U.S. Civil War, the newly invented Winchester Repeating Rifle was used to kill a large number of people. The fortune teller who told Sarah about the future believed that the deaths of her husband and baby were punishment for selling guns that killed so many people.

**Page 15, While You Read**

**WF:** *v.* die/died/will die   *adj.* dead

**Page 17, Talk more about it**

**EXT:** Ask students:
1. What year did carpenters start work on the Winchester House? Use the information in the reading to help you.

2. How many people do you think took care of the house? *Answer: 18–20 servants, 10–22 carpenters, 12–18 gardeners and field hands.*
3. The number 13 is important at the Winchester House. There are 13 bathrooms, 13 steps into one bathroom, and 13 windows in it. In many countries, 13 is an unlucky number. What are unlucky numbers in other countries? Why are they unlucky?

**Page 17, Show you understand**

**PRO:** Point out that the first letter of the first word in each sentence in Part A must change to lower case when it comes after *First, Then,* or *Finally.* For those who need a challenge, introduce *Next* as a synonym for *Then* or other transitional adverbs.

**REF:** http://www.winchestermysteryhouse.com/

### Portrait by a Neighbor

Queen Anne's Lace is a flower (wild carrot).

**Page 19, While You Read**

**EXT:** In small groups have students think about Sarah Winchester and the woman in this poem. How are they the same? How are they different? Then have students write sentences using their lists of ideas.

**REF:** Kazemek, Francis E. and Pat Rigg, *Enriching Our Lives: Poetry Lessons for Adult Literacy Teachers and Tutors*, International Reading Assoc., 1995.

## Unit 4 Food for Thought

**Page 21, Talk About It**

**PRO:**

1. Introduce this page by having students list the fresh, canned, and frozen fruits and vegetables they eat in a *roundtable* activity: Groups of 3–4 students each have a blank piece of paper, and every student has a pencil or pen. When the teacher says go, one student in each group quickly writes a category (e.g. *canned vegetables*) and passes the paper to the next student. That student writes a word in that category and so on, until the teacher calls time. To add a competitive spirit, the group with the most words (or most words that others do not have) wins.

2. Demonstrate how to find information in a graph. Use question 1 in Part A as an example. Students complete the rest of the activity in their groups. Groups should include at least one person who knows how to read graphs and can assist others.

### Greg's Purple Potato Salad

**Page 25, Before You Read**

**PRO:**
A. Skim—Model the activity. Give students about 30 seconds to skim the reading and determine its format.
B. Scan—Model the activity by having students run their fingers down the recipe to look for *15 minutes*. Once students have found it, have them locate the words *boil potatoes*. Show them the example in number 1. Have students complete the exercise. Teachers may wish to provide the times they are scanning for: *10 minutes, 1 minute, 26 minutes.*

**Page 25, While You Read**

**EXT:**
1. Have students rewrite the list of ingredients, abbreviating the measurements.
2. Have students write a recipe for a dish they like and share it with their classmates.

## Unit 5 Comfortable Clothing

### What Will They Think of Next?

**Page 28, While You Read**

**EXT:** Review comparative adjectives. Use *softer*, *more comfortable* from the reading as examples.

**WF:** *v.* fasten    *n.* fastener

**Page 29, Talk more about it**

**EXT:** Have students work in groups to brainstorm interesting uses of Velcro and share their ideas with the class. *Sample answers: to keep a hairpiece on, hair rollers, boots for dogs.*

**Page 30, Write a riddle**

**EXT:** Riddles help develop inference skills. Have students write more riddles using other clothing words in the reading or on another topic. Write a riddle on the board from time to time.

### Jeans Today

**Page 32, Talk more about it**

**EXT:** Discuss the photograph on page 31 in depth and have students discuss why it was hard to buy food and clothing during World War II.

**REF:** http://www.levistrauss.com/

## Unit 6 Heavenly Bodies

### Astronauts in Space

**Page 35, While You Read**

**WF:** *v.* change    *n.* changes    *v.* float    *n.* floating

**Page 36, Talk more about it**

**PRO:** Question 1 can be done as a roundtable activity. See Teacher's Notes for Unit 4, page 21 PRO 1.

**EXT:** Ask students:
1. Would you like to live in space? Why or why not?
2. What would you see? What would you do? Who or what would you miss from earth?

**Page 37, Skim for the purpose**

**PRO:** Model the activity using the example. Give students about 1 minute to complete the exercise.

### Keeping Clean in Space

**Page 38, While You Read**

**PRO:** Point out that items students see in accompanying pictures will often be in readings. Have students match the depicted items with words or phrases in the reading.

**EXT:** To aid comprehension of the word *kit*, show students a real first aid kit.

**WF:** *v.* rinse    *adj.* rinseless (*-less* was introduced in *Words, words, words*, page 37.)

**REF:** http://spacelink.nasa.gov/.index.html Also, books on space in children's sections of libraries.

**Page 40, Read a graph**

**PRO:** see Teacher's Notes for Unit 4, page 21, PRO 2.

## Unit 7 In the Community

### *Mall of America*

#### Page 42, Before You Read

**PRO:** B. Scan—Model the activity using the example. Show students how to run their fingers down the reading to search for the numbers. Give them 2–3 minutes to complete the exercise.

#### Page 43, While You Read

**EXT:** Review superlative adjectives. Use *largest* from the reading as an example.

**WF:** *v.* shop   *n.* shoppers

#### Page 45, Write

**PRO:** Review adverbs of frequency: *always, usually, often, sometimes, never* before students write.

### *Problems in Malls*

#### Page 48, Talk more about it and Write

**PRO:** Both activities include a problem-solving technique: identify the problem, identify possible solutions, and choose a solution. First, limit the students to what they can find in the reading. Later they can bring their experience to the activity.

**EXT:**
1. Discuss possible consequences of the solutions before choosing one.
2. Have students discuss problems and solutions from their own experience.
3. Introduce a different slant or problem, e.g. What do teens dislike about malls?

**REF:** http://www.mallofamerica.com/

## Unit 8 Going Places

#### Page 49, Talk About It

**PRO:** This can be done as a roundtable activity. See Teacher's Notes for Unit 4, page 21, PRO 1.

### *A New World of Transportation*

#### Page 50, While You Read

**EXT:** Review comparative and superlative adjectives. Use adjectives from the reading as examples.

#### Page 51, Talk more about it

**EXT:** Ask students: Would you like to live in a city 125 miles wide? Why or why not?

**REF:** *Odyssey Magazine.* May 1998, vol. 7, issue 5.

### *Poetry in Motion*

#### Page 54, Talk more about it

**EXT:** Other cities such as Toronto and Boston are considering putting poems in public transportation. Ask students: Are there poems on buses or subways in your town?

## Unit 9 School Days

### *A Different Child*

#### Page 56, Before You Read

**PRO:** B. Scan—Model the activity. Show students how to run their fingers down the reading to search for the numbers. Give them about 2 minutes to complete the exercise.

#### Page 59, Skim for the main idea

**PRO:** Model the activity using the example. Give students 2–3 minutes to complete the exercise.

#### Page 59, Write

**EXT:** Review paragraph form. Have students put their sentences in a paragraph with a topic sentence, e.g. Michael is different from other children.

### *Circus School*

#### Page 60, While You Read

**EXT:** Use superlative adjectives (*biggest, most popular*) and the suffix *-less* (*weightless*) for review and reinforcement.

#### Page 62, Write and read

**EXT:** Bring in brochures from local adult schools or other community programs for students to use as a basis for writing.

**REF:** http://www.sfcircus.org/

## Unit 10 Amazing Animals

### Alex, Koko

#### Pages 65–67

These readings are a *jigsaw*, an activity in which some students read one reading and other students read another. Jigsaw activities encourage authentic communication by giving students a reason to read and share the information they have read and to get information from others. (Teachers who prefer not to use the jigsaw format can have all students complete the readings and activities in the order they appear.)

**PRO:** Encourage half the students to read the first reading and the other half to read the second reading. They will all eventually read both stories. Move all the students who are reading one story to the same side of the room so they can help each other if there are questions.

Once the students have read their story, they answer the *Read again* questions (Part A) with a partner who read the same story. Then each pair finds a pair from the other side of the room who read the other story. The students in one pair take turns asking the other pair the questions to complete the chart (*Read again*, Part B).

**EXT:** The dialog between Dr. Patterson and Koko has been translated from American Sign Language to English. ASL is commonly translated like this without correct grammar. Ask students if the conversation uses correct grammar. Ask them to identify the parts that are not correct and rewrite the dialogue using correct grammar.

#### Page 68, Write

**EXT:** Have students put their sentences in paragraph form. Suggest possible topic sentences:
1. Alex and Koko are alike in some ways.
2. Alex and Koko are different in some ways.

Point out that in English the pronouns *he* and *she* are used for male and female animals.

**REF:**
Write to: Gorilla Foundation, P.O. Box 620-640, Woodside, CA 94062, USA
http://www.gorilla.org/index2.html

Write to: The ALEX Foundation, Dr. Irene Pepperberg, Department of Ecology and Evolutionary Biology, University of Arizona, Tucson, AZ 85721, USA
http://www.cages.org/research/pepperberg/index.html

## Unit 11 Working Smart

### How to Find an Occupation You Love

#### Page 72, While You Read

**REF:** http://www.pbs.org/jobs/

#### Page 73, Show you understand

**EXT:** Have students retell Ming's story to a partner.

#### Page 73, Talk more about it

**EXT:** Ask students:
1. Would you follow the steps Ming took to find an occupation? Why or why not?
2. How do people choose an occupation in your country?
3. How do people find a job in your country?

### Dream Benefits

#### Page 76, Read again

**EXT:** Ask students: Does your job have benefits? If yes, what kind? How do these benefits help you?

## Unit 12 Good Sports

### Babe's Early Life, Babe's Dream Comes True

#### Pages 79–81

**PRO:** *Jigsaw* reading. See Teacher's Notes for Unit 10, pages 65–67, PRO. In this unit students work in pairs on *Show you understand* rather than *Read again*.

**EXT:** Use comparative (*far-farther*) and superlative (*greatest, best*) adjectives from the reading for review and reinforcement.

#### Page 81, Show you understand

**PRO:** A. Model the activity using the example. Give students 2–3 minutes to complete the exercise.

**EXT:** B. Have students tell Babe's story to a different partner using the time line to help.

# ANSWER KEY

**Please note:** Answers are not given for prediction or opinion questions.

## Unit 1

### Talk About It [page 1]

A. 1. b    2. a    3. b

### *The Smell of Bread*

#### Read again [page 3]

1. yes    2. no    3. no    4. yes    5. yes    6. no

#### Show you understand [page 3]

2    The baker wants money…
5    The judge says…
3    Gabriel doesn't want…
1    Gabriel smells…
4    Gabriel and the baker ask…

#### Words, words, words [page 4]

1. delicious a,    wonderful a
2. stealing b
3. shake b,    jingle a

### *You Are a Winner*

#### Read again [page 6]

1. b    2. a    3. b    4. b    5. a    6. b

## Unit 2

### Talk About It [page 7]

A.

| Matthew and Melvin | |
|---|---|
| hair | same |
| clothing | same |
| height | same |
| weight | same |

| Jennifer and Jill | |
|---|---|
| hair | different |
| clothing | different |
| height | same |
| weight | same |

### *Two of a Kind*

#### What did you read? [page 9]

a

#### Read again [page 9]

1. same
2. same
3. different
4. different first names, same last names
5. same

#### Show you understand [page 9]

1. They have the same hair color.
2. They have the same eye color.
3. They have the same furniture.
4. They have the same number of children.
5. And they have the same hobby.

#### Skim for the topic [page 10]

1—Physical Description
2—Houses
3—Family
4—Hobbies and Activities

### *A Double Wedding*

#### Read again [page 12]

1. yes    2. yes    3. yes    4. no    5. no

#### Show you understand [page 12]

Ann and her **twin** sister planned a **double** wedding. Ann was **engaged** to a law student, but she **married** the manager of a hat department. Ann's sister is still married, but Ann got **divorced**.

## Unit 3

### *Sarah Winchester and the Mystery House*

#### Read again [page 17]

1. yes    2. no    3. no    4. yes    5. no

#### Show you understand [page 17]

A. 1    Sarah and William got married.
5    Sarah moved west.
3    The baby died.
6    She built a house.
2    They had a baby.
4    William died.

## Pronouns [page 18]

1. He → William Winchester
2. They → Sarah and William
3. She → Sarah
4. It → house
5. They → stairways

## Puzzle [page 18]

1. upset
2. stairways
3. future
4. daughter
5. chimneys
6. gun
7. mystery

Secret word: strange

### Portrait by a Neighbor

## Read again [page 20]

1. a   2. b   3. b   4. a   5. b

## Show you understand [page 20]

I. done, sun
II. lock, o'clock
III. spoon, moon
IV. place, lace

# Unit 4

## Talk About It [page 21]

A. 1. $5.00   2. $2.00   3. $.50   4. $7.50

### Fresh is Best

## What did you read? [page 23]

b

## Read again [page 23]

1. yes   2. no   3. no   4. yes   5. yes

## Show you understand [page 23]

1. Farmers' Markets
2. Farmers' Markets
3. Supermarkets
4. Supermarkets
5. Farmers' Markets

## Words, words, words [page 24]

1. c   2. a   3. b   4. f   5. d   6. e

## Before You Read [page 25]

B. 1. 15 minutes
   2. 10 minutes
   3. 1 minute
   4. 26 minutes

### Greg's Purple Potato Salad

## Read again [page 26]

1. a   2. a   3. b   4. b   5. a   6. b

## Words, words, words [page 26]

1. a   2. b   3. a   4. b   5. a

# Unit 5

### What Will They Think of Next?

## What did you read? [page 29]

b

## Read again [page 29]

1. b   2. a   3. b   4. b   5. a

## Show you understand [page 29]

CLOTHING
swimming trunks        shorts
pants                  jumpsuits

SHOES AND ACCESSORIES
sandals                caps
athletic shoes         backpacks
ties

FASTENERS
buttons                shoelaces
snaps                  rope
zippers                Velcro fasteners
buckles

## Guess the riddle [page 30]

1. a buckle
2. pants or shorts
3. a jumpsuit
4. swimming trunks
5. shoelaces
6. sandals

### Jeans Today

## Read again [page 32]

1. no   2. no   3. no   4. no   5. yes   6. yes   7. yes

# Unit 6

## Talk About It [page 33]

A. 1. blood pressure
   2. heart
   3. lungs
   4. muscles
   5. bones

## Astronauts in Space

### Read again [page 36]

I. A. taller
   B. smaller
   C. bones, muscles
   D. toothache
II. A. motion
   B. stand, walk

### Skim for the purpose [page 37]

1—begins the article
2—tells about changes in the body
3—tells about changes in the brain
4—ends the article

### Words, words, words [page 37]

B. 1. weightless
   2. sleepless
   3. tasteless
   4. skinless, boneless
   5. rinseless

## Keeping Clean in Space

### What did you read? [page 39]

Astronauts must keep clean in space.

### Read again [page 39]

1. b   2. b   3. a   4. b   5. a   6. b

### Read a graph [page 40]

A. 1. 8 1/2 hours
   2. 2 1/2 hours
   3. 1 1/2 hours
   4. 1 1/2 hours
   5. 2
   6. work

## Unit 7

### Before You Read [page 42]

B. 1. 900,000
   2. 7
   3. 29
   4. 27
   5. $650 million
   6. 100,000

## Mall of America

### Read again [page 44]

1. no   2. yes   3. no   4. yes   5. no   6. no   7. yes

### Show you understand [page 44]

Mall of America is very **large**. It is the largest **mall** in the United States. It is like a small **city**. The mall has a bank and a **post office**. It has many stores and **restaurants**. It has entertainment, too. You can go to a **movie** or play miniature **golf**. You can even go to an **amusement park** and ride a roller coaster.

### Words, words, words [page 45]

1. c   2. a   3. d   4. e   5. f   6. b

## Problems in Malls

### Read again [page 47]

1. yes   2. yes   3. yes   4. no   5. no   6. yes

## Unit 8

### A New World of Transportation

### What did you read [page 51]

b

### Read again [page 51]

1. will change
2. 700
3. expensive
4. 4 times
5. may
6. work

### Show you understand [page 51]

1. High-speed planes
2. High-speed trains
3. New large planes
4. High-speed trains
5. High-speed planes
6. High-speed planes

### Outline [page 52]

I. A. 600–800 passengers
   B. bigger and faster
   C. very expensive
II. A. more than 300 mph
   B. the first countries to use the high-speed trains
III. A New World
   A. to live in one city and work in another
   B. in a very large city 125 miles wide

### Poetry in Motion

### Read again [page 54]

1. yes   2. no   3. yes   4. no   5. no   6. yes

# Unit 9

## Talk About It [page 55]

A. 1. yes    2. yes    3. no    4. yes    5. no

## Before You Read [page 56]

B. 5 years old—high school
6 years old—community college
10 years old—university
12 years old—graduate school

## *A Different Child*

### Read again [page 58]

1. a    2. b    3. b    4. a    5. b    6. b

### Show you understand [page 58]

Michael Kearney is very **smart**. He began to **read** when he was 8 months old. At age 5 he went to **high school**. It was too easy for him so he studied at **home**. His mother was his **teacher**. At age 10 he graduated from a **university**. At age 12 he got his Master's **degree**.

### Skim for the main idea [page 59]

1—Schooling in the United States
2—Michael's early schooling
3—Michael's college days
4—Michael's future

### Words, words, words [page 59]

1. a    2. b    3. b    4. a    5. a

## *Circus School*

### Read again [page 61]

1. yes    2. no    3. yes    4. no    5. yes

### Words, words, words [page 61]

1. c    2. d    3. a    4. b

# Unit 10

## Talk About It [page 63]

A. LAND ANIMALS
   gorilla    cat    dog    horse    wolf
   lion    chimpanzee

SEA ANIMALS
   whale    seal    fish    dolphin

BIRDS
   owl    parrot    rooster

INSECTS
   bee    grasshopper

## *Alex and Koko*

### Read again [page 67]

A. and B. *(answers may vary)*

|     | Alex | Koko |
| --- | --- | --- |
| 1. | parrot | gorilla |
| 2. | English | American Sign Language |
| 3. | more than 100 | more than 1,000 |
| 4. | Dr. Irene Pepperberg; she wants to find out how parrots' brains work | Dr. Penny Patterson; she wants to know if gorillas are like humans |
| 5. | name 40 objects, 5 shapes, 4 materials, and 7 colors; answer questions; solve problems; ask for food | ask and answer questions; talk about the past and future; use a computer and a camera; tell when she feels happy or sad |

## Pronouns [page 68]

1. they → animals
2. She → Dr. Irene Pepperberg
3. he → Alex
4. it → tray
5. they → gorillas

## *Gorilla Saves Boy*

### Read again [page 70]

1. yes    2. no    3. yes    4. yes    5. yes

### Puzzle [page 70]

DOWN
1. climbed
2. hero
3. dangerous

ACROSS
1. cheered
4. landed
5. gently
6. wrong

# Unit 11

## *How to Find an Occupation You Love*

### Read again [page 73]

1. a    2. b    3. a    4. b    5. b    6. b

## Show you understand [page 73]

<u>1</u>   She thought about…
<u>5</u>   She chose one place…
<u>3</u>   She chose one occupation.
<u>2</u>   She made a list…
<u>4</u>   She looked for the names…
<u>7</u>   She volunteered…
<u>6</u>   She called and talked…

## Words, words, words [page 74]

1. c   2. e   3. d   4. a   5. b

### *Dream Benefits*

## What did you read? [page 76]

A happy worker does a good job.

## Read again [page 76]

*(answers may vary)*

| Benefit | Saves time | Saves money | Keeps workers healthy | Keeps workers happy |
|---|---|---|---|---|
| 1. childcare center | X | X | | X |
| 2. park | | | | X |
| 3. cafeteria | X | X | | |
| 4. health club/ health insurance | | X | X | X |
| 5. medical clinic/ dental clinic | X | X | X | |

# Unit 12

### *Babe's Early Life*

## Read again [page 79]

1. no   2. yes   3. yes   4. no   5. yes   6. no

### *Babe's Dream Comes True*

## Read again [page 80]

1. b   2. b   3. b   4. a   5. b   6. b

## Show you understand [page 81]

A. and B.

BABE'S EARLY LIFE

1911  Babe was born.
1931  Babe led her team to win a basketball championship.
1930  Babe competed in her first track and field meet.
1930  Babe began to play basketball on a company team.

BABE'S DREAM COMES TRUE

1950  Newspapers called Babe the "greatest female athlete."
1932  Babe won three Olympic track and field medals.
1946  Babe won 17 golf tournaments in a row.
1932  Babe won five events at a national track and field meet.

## Words, words, words [page 82]

1. c   2. a   3. d   4. e   5. b

### *TV Sports Fans*

## Read again [page 84]

1. no   2. no   3. yes   4. yes   5. yes   6. yes

## Show you understand [page 84]

People like to watch **sports** on TV. The most **popular** sport in the world is soccer. **Fans** get together in their homes and outside to watch their **team** play. The fans **cheer** and shout when their team scores. When their team **wins**, they celebrate.

# WORD LIST

Here are the words from *Read All About It 1* that are in *The Oxford Picture Dictionary*. To find a word in this list, look for the title of the reading where you saw the word, and then find the word under the title. The first number after each word refers to the page in *The Oxford Picture Dictionary* where you can find the word. The second number (or letter) refers to the item on that page.

the word          the page number of *The Oxford Picture Dictionary*

brown    **12**–11

the number (or letter) of the item in *The Oxford Picture Dictionary*

If only the **bold** page number appears, that word is part of the unit title or subtitle or is somewhere else on the page.

The words in the list are in the form you see in the reading. When the word in the list has a very different form from the word in the *Dictionary*, you will see the *Dictionary* word next to it (pennies   penny   **20**–1). When the word in the reading is used as a different part of speech from the word in the *Dictionary*, the part of speech appears after the word in the list.

*n.* = noun; *v.* = verb; *adv.* = adverb; *adj.* = adjective

Words in the list that are in **bold** type are verbs or verb phrases.

---

## Unit 1 Money Troubles

### *The Smell of Bread, page 2*

angry    **31**–29
**answers**    **6**–H
**asks**    **6**–G
baker    **136**–8
bakery    **89**–16
bread    **54**–29
brown    **12**–11
**buy**    **21**–C
coins    **20**
day    **18**–10
difficult    **11**–24
**eating**    **60**-A
every day    **18**–21
hours    **16**–3
in front of    **13**–4
judge    **99**–6
**listens**    **2**–C
little    **11**–1
**lives**    **116**–B
man    **22**–11

money    **20**
morning    **17**–16
**pays for**    **21**–C
pennies    penny    **20**–1
problem    **11**–24
**says**    **6**–C
**sees**    **75**–A
**sits down**    **2**–E
small town    **34**–3
**smells**    **75**–C
ten    **14**
thick    **11**–7
two    **14**
winter *adj.*    **19**–40

### *You Are A Winner! page 5*

angry    **31**–29
birthday    **19**–41
boxes    **11**–13
car    **106**
check    **20**–14
color *adj.*    **12**
cost    **21**–6

credit card   **20**–15
**dials** the number   **9**–D
dolls   **45**–18
evening   **17**–19
excited   **31**–23
expensive   **11**–19
**gets** home   **27**–Q
girl   **22**–5
**give**   **21**–D
happy   **31**–32
in   **13**–5
inch   **15**–13
jewelry   **69**–8
light   **11**–14
little   **11**–1
long–distance call   **9**–5
**looks at**   **111**–K
mail   **96**
mailbox   **38**–4
money   **20**
next week   **18**–20
number   **14**
**opens**   **2**–I
**paid   pay**   **21**–C
**pay**   **21**–C
phone   **9**–1
postcard   **96**–3
**says**   **6**–C
sending *n.*   **send**   **96**–B
surprised   **31**–31
telephone number   **4**–11
toy   **94**–5
TV   **42**–26
two   **14**
wife   **24**–20
**win**   **158**
woman   **22**–10

## Unit 2  Seeing Double

*Two of a Kind, page 8*

addresses   **4**–5
average height   **22**–17
black hair   **23**–15
brothers   **24**–9
brown   **12**–11
children   **22**–1
clothing   **64–67**
**collect**   **162**–A
**cook** dinner   **27**–P
cousins   **24**–12
dolls   **45**–18
eyes   **74**–27
faces   **74**
furniture   **35**–K
floor plan   **38**–1

glasses   **81**–35
**go** to the market   **26**–L
hobby   hobbies   **162–163**
houses   **34**–6
husbands   **24**–19
lonely   **30**–18
married   **25**–23
middle-aged   **22**–14
names   **4**–1
next to   **13**–1
shopping   **21**
short   **23**–1
sisters   **24**–8
tin·e   **16–17**
twice a week   **18**–23
wavy   **23**–10
weekends   **18**–13
weight   **22**–21

*A Double Wedding, page 11*

attractive   **22**–23
beautiful   **11**–21
**buy**   **21**–C
day   **18**–10
department store   **93**–13
**divorced** *v.*   **25**–24
excited   **31**–23
**fell in love   fall in love**   **28**–K
**get married**   **28**–L
hands   **74**–8
hat *adj.*   **66**–1
husband   **24**–19
interesting   **167**–30
July   **19**–31
life   **28–29**
manager   **54**–8
**married** *v.*   **25**–23
Minnesota   **122–123**
new   **71**–32
**planned**   **169**–A
sister   **24**–8
student   **2**–3
university   **112**–10

## Unit 3  Home Sweet Home

*Sarah Winchester and the Mystery House, page 15*

**asked**   **6**–G
baby   **22**–2
bedrooms   **44**
big   **11**–2
**bought   buy**   **21**–C
**build** (see construction)   **149**
California   **122–123**
carpenters   **48**–12

ceiling **42**–5
chimneys **38**–21
Connecticut **122–123**
daughter **24**–21
days **18**–10
**died** **29**–R
doors **38**–11
every day **18**–21
family **24–25**
**fell in love** **fall in love** **28**–K
fireplaces **42**–9
**got married** **get married** **28**–L
gun **100**–9
happy **31**–32
**had** a baby **have** a baby **29**–M
hours **16**–3
house **34**–6
husband **24**–19
kitchens **40**
life *n.* **28–29**
little **11**–1
**move** **29**–P
mystery **166**–15
**open** **2**–I
**packed** (see **unpack**) **35**–E
sad **31**–20
**said** **say** **6**–C
scared **31**–24
sick **30**–14
small town **34**–3
son **24**–22
stairways **37**–26
tuberculosis **79**–13
upset **31**–30
walls **42**–6
warm **10**–2
west **107, 123**
windows **38**–17
woman **22**–10
year **18**–8

## *Portrait by a Neighbor, page 19*

chimney **38**–21
day **18**–10
dishes **41**–2
floor **44**–24
garden (see yard) **39**
key **37**–31
lawn **39**–21
lettuce **51**–1
lock **37**–29
meadow **117**–20
midnight **17**–21
moon **127**–13—16
**mows** **39**–C
**see** **75**–A

shovel **39**–13
spoon **41**–23
sun **127**–10
**swept** **sweep** **46**–E
ten o'clock **16**
**weeds** **39**–A

## Unit 4 Food for Thought

### *Fresh is Best, page 22*

apples **50**–4
big **11**–2
business people (see business man/business
   woman) **136**–10
**buying** **21**–C
canned **54**–4
carrots **51**–3
cauliflower **51**–16
cheaper **11**–20
cities city **34**–1
fall **19**–39
farm **34**–13
farmers **148**–15
fresh **53**–29
frozen **53**–30
fruit **50**
**looking** **141**–B
markets **54**
**moved** **29**–P
music **120**
packaged foods **56**
**playing** **120**–A
potatoes **51**–21
prices **21**–6
produce **54**–11
purple **12**–7
raspberries **50**–18
ripe **50**–29
**selling** **21**–B
**shopped** **21**–A
smell *n.* **smell** **75**–C
suburbs **34**–2
sun **127**–10
**talk** **2**–B
**tasting** **taste** **75**–D
today **18**–5
towns **34**–3
United States **122–123**
vegetables **51**
**walking** **101**–A
white **12**–14
World War II **114**
years **18**–8
yellow **12**–12

## Greg's Purple Potato Salad, page 25

add **58**–Q
**boil** **58**–P
bowl **59**–31
chopped *adj.* **chop** **58**–G
colander **59**–17
cold water **43**–7
cook **137**–17
cup **57**–10
**cut** (see **cut up**) **58**–M
family **24–25**
farm **34**–13
farmer **148**–15
fresh **53**–29
frozen **53**–30
ingredients **58**–K
minutes **16**–2
**mix** **58**–K
paper towel **40**–2
parsley **51**–10
peas **51**–19
pepper **41**–15
potato salad **53**–13
potatoes **51**–21
pound **57**–12
purple **12**–7
quarts **57**–4
**rinse** **76**–F
salad dressing **60**–18
salt **57**–6
saucepan **59**–25
small **70**–2
soft **11**–6
surprised **31**–31
tablespoons **57**–7
time **16**
teaspoon **57**–6
vegetables **51**
wooden spoon **59**–9

## Unit 5 Comfortable Clothing

### What Will They Think of Next, page 28

astronauts **127**–17
athletic shoes **68**–23
backpacks **69**–28
boys' *adj.* **22**–4
buckles **69**–41
buttons **73**–21
caps **66**–6
clothing **64–67**
country **34**–4
difficult **11**–24
dog **133**–11
engineer **137**–23
easier **easy** **11**–23

every day **18**–21
fields (see meadow) **117**–20
fur **134**–19
**get dressed** **26**–D
hooks **150**–34
jumpsuits **65**–16
material **70**
microscope **199**–4
pants **64**–8
pockets **73**–4
rope **154**–19
sandals **68**–24
seeds **129**–1
**sell** **21**–B
shoelaces **68**–14
shorts **64**–13
space **127**–22
swimming trunks **66**–22
ties **69**–10
waist **74**–4
**walk** **101**–A
weed *n.* **weed** **39**–A
years **18**–8
zippers **73**–16

### Jeans Today, page 31

Africa **124**–5
Asia **125**–4
baggy **71**–42
**broke** **break** **82**–F
**buy** **21**–C
clothing **64–67**
comfortable **30**–7
cotton **70**–16
**cut** **23**–A
dark blue **12**–2
day **18**–10
Europe **125**–3
evening gowns **65**–29
food **58**
formal **71**–36
hard **11**–24
hats **68**–5
**heard** **hear** **75**–B
hospital **87**
**hurt** **82**–A
jackets **66**–7
jeans **64**–5
leg **74**–6
man **22**–11
material **70**
millions **14**
minutes **16**–2
North America **124**–1
nurse **87**–22
overalls **65**–21
pain **30**–12

plaid **70**–9
**pull** **153**–A
**said** **say** **6**–C
**sent** **send** **96**–B
shorts **64**–13
skirts **64**–10
softer **11**–6
striped **70**–7
suits **64**–2
tight **71**–43
tuxedos **65**–28
war **114**
**wash** **72**
world **124**–125
year **18**–8

## Unit 6  Heavenly Bodies

### *Astronauts in Space, page 35*

astronauts **127**–17
blood **79**–15
body **75**–75
bones **75**–49
brains **75**–35
cold **30**–4
days **18**–10
dental fillings **84**–22
dentists **84**–18
difficult **11**–24
earth **127**–7
every day **18**–21
**exercise** **27**–W
first **14**
headaches **78**–1
heads **74**–1
hearts **75**–38
inches **15**–13
into. **105**–4
**leave** **111**–L
minutes **16**–2
muscles **75**–48
nausea *n.* (see **feel** nauseous) **78**–D
planets **127**
sickness *n.* sick **30**–14
skin **75**–51
space **127**–22
stars **127**–23
**studying** **6**–7
symptoms **78**
taller **22**–16
teeth **75**–25
toothache **78**–2
under **13**–9
vomiting *n.* **vomit** **78**–E
**walk** **101**–A

### *Keeping Clean in Space, page 38*

body lotion **76**–7
brush **76**–14
**brush**…teeth **77**–J
clean **72**–16
comb **76**–13
**cut**…nails **77**–N
deodorant **76**–4
difficult **11**–24
**dry**…hair **76**–H
good **11**–17
hair **74**–19
nail clippers **77**–29
personal hygiene **76**–77
shampoo **76**–9
slowly *adv.* slow **11**–4
soap **76**–2
**take** a bath **76**–B
**take** a shower **76**–A
toothbrush **77**–20
toothpaste **77**–21
towel **43**–8
**wash**…hair **76**–E
washcloths **43**–14
water **155**–1
wet **72**–17

## Unit 7  In the Community

### *Mall of America, page 43*

adult school **112**–8
amusement park **152**–13
bank **88**–3
baseball *adj.* **158**–9
bookstores **92**–4
**build** (see construction) **149**
building **34**–5
city **34**–1
Canada **122**–125
clothing *adj.* **64**–67
dental clinic **84**
department stores **93**–13
electronics stores **93**–18
entertainment **166**–167
fast food restaurants **90**–14
fish **130**
florists **92**–12
gallons **57**–5
golf **159**–7
hair salons **93**–16
high school **112**–7
hungry **30**–5
Japan **122**–125
mall **92**–93
medical clinic **84**
Minnesota **122**–123

movie theater    **88**–11
music stores    **92**–1
paint    **151**–20
places    **152**
post office    **89**–29
restaurants    **90**–14
roller coaster    **152**–15
schools    **112**
screen    **165**–28
**see**    **75**–A
shoe stores    **92**–10
**shop**    **21**–A
small    **34**–3
stadiums    **152**–26
stores    **92**–93
travel agencies    travel agency    **92**–9
United Kingdom    **124**–125
United States    **122**–125
university    **112**–10
world    **124**–125

### Problems in Malls, page 47

adult    **22**–9
angry    **31**–29
**arrest**    **99**–A
children    **22**–1
church *adj.*    **88**–6
family *adj.*    **24**–25
**go** to court  (see **appear** in court)    **99**–C
**handcuff** *v.*    handcuffs    **99**–2
**hired**    **141**–L
illegal drugs    **100**–4
lights  (see light fixture)    **41**–5
malls    **92**–93
manager    **54**–8
new    **71**–32
parents    **24**–4
parking garage    **89**–26
**planned**    **169**–A
police officers    **99**–1
problems    **11**–24
Saturdays    **18**–7
**says**    **6**–C
scared    **31**–24
security guards    **97**–4
**shop**    **21**–A
store owners    **139**–56
teenagers    **22**–6
weekends    **18**–13

## Unit 8  Going Places

### A New World of Transportation, page 50

airplanes    **110**–9
bigger    **11**–2
**carry**    **62**–H
cars    **106**

city    **34**–1
comfortable    **30**–7
expensive    **11**–19
faster    **11**–3
Germany    **124**–125
horses    **133**–4
hours    **16**–3
Japan    **124**–125
**live**    **116**–B
miles    **15**
minutes    **16**–2
new    **71**–32
passengers    **104**–7
planes    **111**
Switzerland    **124**–125
ticket    **104**–14
trains    **104**–17
transportation    **104**
**travel**    **29**–N
**use**    **140**–N
wide    **71**–44
**work**    **26**–K
world    **124**–125

### Poetry in Motion, page 53

across    **105**–3
ages    **22**
bus    **104**–4
every day    **18**–21
ferries    ferry    **104**–23
happy    **31**–32
home    **27**–Q
**listen to**    **2**–C
magazines    **98**–7
music    **120**
newspapers    **98**–8
night    **17**–20
passengers    **104**–7
planes    **111**
public transportation    **104**
railroad    **107**–11
**read**    **6**–B
**ride**    **91**–E
school    **89**–27
see    **75**–A
soft    **11**–6
subway    **104**–9
**talk**    **7**–P
trains    **104**–17
traveling *n.*    **travel**    **29**–N
walls    **42**–6
window    **38**–17
work *n.*    **work**    **26**–K
world    **124**–125
**wrote**    write    **113**–A
year    **18**–8

## Unit 9  School Days

### A Different Child, page 57

actor  **136**–2
algebra  **118**–25
Bachelor's degree  **112**
**began  begin  8**–B
bored  **31**–26
child  children  **22**–1
college  **112**–10
community college  **112**
earth  **127**–7
easy  **11**–23
elementary school  **112**–5
game show  **167**–23
geography  **117**
**graduate  28**–D
graduate school  **112**
high school  **112**–7
**left  leave  111**–L
Master's degree  **112**
mother  **24**–5
preschool  **112**–4
**read  6**–B
**studied  study  6**–7
**studying  6**–7
**taught  teach**  (see teacher *n.*)  **5**–2
television *adj.*  **42**–26
United States  **124**–125
university  **112**–10
vocational school  **112**–9
year  **18**–8

### Circus School, page 60

Australia  **124**–125
Bachelor's degree  **112**
biggest  **11**–2
blind  **22**–26
Canada  **124**–125
careful  **147**–24
college  **112**–10
doctors  **84**–6
economics  **121**–6
elementary school *adj.*  **112**–5
England  **124**–125
evening  **17**–19
feeling  **30**–31
hairdressers  **137**–30
high school *adj.*  **112**–7
man  **22**–11
physically challenged  **22**–5
**received  96**–D
scared  **31**–24
school  **112**
**stop  165**–F
students  **139**–57
teachers  **139**–58

teaches  teach  **140**  (see also teacher *n.*)  **5**–2
through  **105**–11
United States  **122**–125
world  **124**–125

## Unit 10  Amazing Animals

### Alex, page 65

animals  **133**
**answer  6**–H
**asks  6**–G
balls  **45**–16
birdie  bird  **132**
blue  **12**–1
brains  **75**–35
colors  **12**
cubes  **118**–10
feelings  **30**–31
**gives  21**–D
good  **11**–17
green  **12**–8
interesting  **167**–30
name  **4**–1
nut  **50**–23
plastic  **70**
red  **12**–13
**say  6**–C
shapes  **118**
**speak  140**–J
square  **118**–6
**studying  6**–7
talk  **141**–A
**taught  teach**  (see teacher *n.*)  **5**–2
tray  **41**–10
wood  **149**–17

### Koko, page 66

animals  **133**
**answer  6**–H
**ask  6**–G
bad  **11**–18
camera  **165**–24
child  children  **22**–1
computer  **144**
deaf  **22**–27
feelings  **30**–31
gorilla  **135**–30
hands  **74**–8
happy  **31**–32
interesting  **167**–30
pound  **57**–12
sad  **31**–20
sorry  (see **apologize**)  **8**–I
**speak  140**–J
**studies**  (see studying)  **6**–7
**studying  6**–7

talk **7**–P
**taught** **teach** (see teacher *n.*) **5**–2
tools **150**–151
**use** **140**–N

### Gorilla Saves Boy, page 69

August **19**–32
baby **22**–2
big **11**–2
boy **22**–4
**carried** **carry** **62**–H
**climbed** **153**–C
dangerous **147**–8
every day **18**–21
excited **31**–23
**fell** **fall** **82**–O
gorillas **135**–30
**got up** **get up** **26**–B
head **74**–1
large **70**–4
**live** **116**–B
mother **24**–5
near **13**
**opened** **2**–I
**picked up** **94**–G
relieved **30**–16
rocks **155**–24
scared **31**–24
**see** **75**–A
surprised **31**–31
**touched** **75**–E
**walked** **156**–A
**watching** **27**–5
worried **30**–13
zoo **152**–1
zookeeper **152**–3

## Unit 11 Working Smart

### How to Find an Occupation You Love, page 72

**asked** **6**–G
counselor **5**–16
days **18**–10
degree **29**–7
**filled out** applications **141**–G
**gave** **give** **21**–D
good **11**–17
**go to college** **28**–J
hired (see **get hired**) **141**–L
information (see **call** for information) **141**–E
interesting **167**–30
job **136**–138
lawyer **138**–36
**listen** **2**–C
**look at** the job board **141**–B

**look in** the classifieds **141**–D
months **19**
nurse **138**–42
occupations **136**–138
police officer **138**–44
problems **11**–24
receptionist **138**–47
**said** **say** **6**–C
salary (see **inquire** about the salary) **141**–K
salesperson **139**–50
school **89**–27
**see** **75**–A
summer **19**–38
**talk** **7**–P
teacher **139**–58
telephone **9**–1
telephone book **9**–15
volunteers **87**–19
week **18**–24
**work** **26**–K
**write** **113**–A

### Dream Benefits, page 75

beautiful **11**–21
benefits **141**–J
building **34**–5
cafeteria **5**–4
caregivers **136**–12
childcare center **94**–95
children **11**–11
**close** **2**–J
construction workers **149**–1
cooks **137**–17
dentist **137**–20
doctor **137**–22
eyes **74**–27
**exercise** **157**–P
flowers **129**
food **58**
gardeners **137**–26
happy **31**–32
health club **89**–21
in front of **13**–4
insurance **84**–4/5
large **70**–4
lawn **39**–21
life **28**–29
lunch **61**
medical clinic **84**
money **20**
**mowing** **39**–C
music **120**
musicians **138**–41
noon **17**–17
office building **89**–24
park **88**–8
**planting** **148**–A

play    120–A
see    75–A
sick    30–14
take a walk  (see walk)    156–A
toothache    78–2
windows    38–17
work    26–K

## Unit 12  Good Sports

### Babe's Early Life, page 79

baseball adj.    158–9
basketball    158–8
began    begin    8–B
boys    22–4
football    161–22
game    152–18
get hurt  (see be hurt)    82–A
high school    112–7
hired    141–L
hit    156–G
jumped    156–J
kick    156–L
name    4–2
neighborhood    90
play    162–B
player    158–5
ran    run    156–C
scored    158–1
secretary    142–3
sports    158–160
swimming adj.    swim    157–T
team    158–3
tennis adj.    159–14
track and field    159–17
volleyball adj.    158–14
was born    be born    28–A
win    158
women    woman    22–10
work    26–K
years    18–8

### Babe's Dream Comes True, page 80

baseball    158–9
basketball    158–8
began    begin    8–B
billiards    159–2
bowling    159–3
female    4–14
first place    152–20
get hurt  (see be hurt)    82–A
golf    159–7
helped    6–J
hours    16–3
jumped    156–J

jumping adj.    jump    156–J
newspapers    98–8
play    162–B
ran    run    158–C
running adj.    run    156–C
sports    158–160
teenager    22–6
tennis    159–14
throwing adj.    throw    156–D
track and field    159–17
week    18–11
women    woman    22–10
won    win    158
years    18–8

### TV Sports Fans, page 83

Asia    124–125
basketball adj.    158–8
Brazil    124–125
college adj.    112–10
entertainment    166–167
every day    18–21
excited    31–23
families    family    24–25
fans    158–4
faster    11–3
football adj.    158–11
holidays    168
ice skating    160–4
Japan    124–125
lives    life    28–29
martial arts    159–10
New Year's Day    168–1
parties  party    33
programs    167
scores    158–1
shouts n.    shout    169–G
soccer    158–12
South Korea    124–125
sports    158–160
stops    107–3
streets    90–9
Taiwan    124–125
team    158–3
tennis    159–14
Thanksgiving    168–15
TV (television)    164–6
United States    122–125
volleyball    158–14
watch    27–5
week    18–11
win    158
winners n.    win    158
won    win    158
world    124–125

# ⬙ REMEMBER THE WORDS

Learn new words.  Follow the steps to fill in the chart. Study the chart, and you will soon remember the words.

1. **Choose a word you want to remember and write it in the chart.**

2. **Find out how to say the word and write it in a way you can remember.** Ask an English-speaking friend, look in a dictionary, or ask your teacher.

3. **Find out what it means and write the meaning.** Look in the reading for clues. Ask your partner, classmate, family member, or an English-speaking friend. Look in a dictionary or ask your teacher.

4. **Copy the sentence from the reading.**

| UNIT | 1. WHAT IS THE WORD? | 2. HOW DO YOU SAY IT? | 3. WHAT DOES IT MEAN? | 4. SENTENCE FROM THE READING |
|------|------|------|------|------|
| 1 | coins | koynz | money made of metal—penny, dime | Listen to the sound of the coins, Baker. |

| UNIT | 1. WHAT IS THE WORD? | 2. HOW DO YOU SAY IT? | 3. WHAT DOES IT MEAN? | 4. SENTENCE FROM THE READING |
|------|----------------------|------------------------|------------------------|------------------------------|
|      |                      |                        |                        |                              |